C000053882

FIGHTER
FUGITIVE
KING

Also by Fraser Keay

The Abuse of Power and the Grace of God
(e-book and audiobook)

*The Character and Timing
of the Kingdom of God*
(e-book)

The King's Table
(e-book and audiobook)

*Youth Ministry Across the Continents:
Eleven Youth Pastors From Ten Countries On The Key Building Blocks
For Effective Youth Work Leadership In The Local Church*
(paperback, 2nd edition)

*Mentoring Ministry:
How God Can Use You to Shape the Following Generations*
(e-book, paperback and audiobook)

FRASER KEAY

FIGHTER
FUGITIVE
KING

David's Leadership Development,
How It Can Point Men
To Christ,
And Its Relevance Today

FIGHTER, FUGITIVE, KING
David's Leadership Development,
How it Can Point Men to Christ,
and its Relevance Today
© Fraser Keay, 2021
The author asserts the moral right to be identified as the author of this work.

Published by Illumine Press, an imprint of
First Half Leadership Publishing,
United Kingdom

Unless indicated, all Scripture references are taken from THE HOLY BIBLE, NEW INTERNATIONAL VERSION®, NIV® Copyright © 1973, 1978, 1984, 2011 by Biblica, Inc.™ Used by permission. All rights reserved worldwide.

All rights reserved. Except as part of copyright legislation, no part of this publication may be reproduced, stored in a retrieval system, or transmitted in any form or by any means, electronic, mechanical, photocopying or otherwise, without the prior written consent of the publisher. Short extracts may be used for review purposes.

ISBN 978-0-9954729-8-3 (hardback)
ISBN 978-0-9954729-7-6 (paperback)
ISBN 978-0-9954729-4-5 (e-book)

Printed by Ingram and others

A CIP catalogue record for this book is available
from the British library

Email address for all publishing matters:
firsthalfleadership@gmail.com

For Jim Pirie, Mark Taft, Jim Scott
and Rick Cole.

Thank you for the different things each of you
put into me during my 20s and 30s.

Thank you too to my father who proofread the entire manuscript,
and to my wife for her unfailing support.

CONTENTS

COMMENDATIONS

"There is a leadership crisis in the world today and this book is a passionate appeal to Christian men to be leaders who lead like Jesus seen through the lens of the life of David. It is clear, theological, challenging and hugely practical. I would recommend this as a disciple making tool for older men to disciple a younger generation."

**Guy Miller, Leader of Commission
Network of Churches, U.K.**

"There are many good Bible teachers around. There are also plenty of people who can give wisdom about leadership. What is much more rare is finding somebody who can genuinely unlock the Bible and apply it spiritually and practically to Christian leadership today. Fraser Keay is one such person! In this book his passion and experience for developing younger leaders shines through, but it shines through the biblical lens of the life of David and then onto Christ. If you want a book full of trendy leadership cliches then this isn't for you, but if you want to grow as a leader and develop leaders yourself, and want to do so trusting God and relying on Jesus, then read on! I've spent much time in my Christian ministry working with younger leaders, and my only criticism of this book is that Fraser didn't write it 30 years ago – my investment into younger leaders would've been so much stronger if he had!"

**Rev. Nigel James, pastor in the Elim Pentecostal Church Movement,
based in Cardiff, Wales, U.K. and working in the USA
with the Awakening Foundation and around the
world in various mission partnerships.**

INTRODUCTION

THIS BOOK IS primarily for Christian men in the first half of their adult life who aspire to lead, or who already have some sort of leadership responsibility whether in the workplace, church or other ministry context. Older men mentoring those younger may also find it a helpful resource. Also, some of the issues are certainly not confined to the first half of life, e.g. struggling with fear or depression or having to wait patiently for God to fulfil some word or other that you sense he's given you.

If you currently serve as a leader or have aspirations to lead, whatever your sphere of service your first half is a critical period of development. Time and time again in Scripture we see God putting people through a number of tests during different stages of their lives. For those who've become believers at an early age this can be especially true of their first half in life.

Moses, whose life foreshadows Christ who delivered people from slavery to sin, is a good example. He spent 40 years in the desert before being called to lead God's people (Acts 7:23 and Exodus 7:7). God did it with his people too: they spent 40 years in the desert being tested and humbled as an entire generation was wiped out through God's judgment for consistent unbelief (Deuteronomy 1:32-36 and 8:2-5). This foreshadowed the Lord himself who spent 40 days in the desert being tested (Luke 4:1-2 and Matt 4:1). Unlike most of Israel, he did not fail when tempted.

The tests many developing leaders go through, whatever their sphere of influence, are meant to provide important lessons behind the scenes before being thrust into a more advanced role, perhaps in a more public setting exercising leadership upfront, as well as with others behind the scenes. It's often a long season of following others or looking after some small task, or people, while slowly learning to lead. God designs these tests not only to shape our character but to equip us to serve him well in the years to come. For each test he provides grace in various forms to enable us to succeed in doing his will.

While certainly no guarantee of a successful second half of life and leadership, consistently godly responses to such tests, and God's grace to handle these difficulties, help lay a solid foundation for what's to come later, and at the end a rich welcome into the city of the great King (2 Peter 1:1-10).

Like every other king, David ultimately failed to bring in the perfect kingdom God desired; we see his slow decline in 2nd Samuel, but overall he was a man after God's own heart, an epitaph I'm sure any true believer would want (Psalm 78:72; Acts 13:22).

WHY DAVID?

Many reading or listening to this will be familiar with the story about a young lad named David who broke dramatically onto the stage by killing the giant Philistine, Goliath — the biggest and most feared fighter of his day — after a 40-day stand-off between two opposing armies.

David the amateur passed a test that professionally trained soldiers had insufficient faith and power to complete. And remarkably, we have more material about the first half of his life and leadership than just about any other leader in the Bible. The youngest son in his family, he went from watching his father's sheep to having command of a large unit of men in the military, to being on the run for several years to eventually becoming the leader of his country at age 37.

Not only do we have a record of David's adventures (from around 1,000 B.C.), incredibly, we also have his personal diaries from that time period as well: the Psalms. If you just pause and think about that for a moment, even just in literary or historical terms that is in itself staggering – 3,000 year-old journal entries.

Yet David faced arguably greater challenges in his 20s and 30s which we will read about or listen to. In David, we find a man who typically responded in obedience to God's commands, impacted a nation, and established a kingdom. These can yield for us some important lessons about leadership. But it's not the main reason these true stories were written down.

The stories we have about his life are all there to lead us to another king. Setting aside the glories of heaven above with the Father, Jesus came into our world as a baby, and having served an apprenticeship as a carpenter and then helping run the family business he was anointed by his Father above, inaugurated a kingdom, and rendered a service that would eventually lead to his death for all. If everything he did had been written down there would probably not be enough room in the whole world to fit the number of books that could be written (John 21:25). That would be some library.

The Lord's greatest challenge lay at the end of his life. This king-priest 'offered up prayers and petitions with fervent cries and tears to the one who could save him from death, and he was heard because of his reverent submission' (Hebrews 5:7). Unlike David, he was rejected by the nation of Israel he came to serve. He did not come to take up a throne using a sword, but gently lifts up the needy with the sword of his mouth, the proclamation and evidence of the gospel (John 6:15 and 18:36). In Matthew chapter 12 verses 15-21 it says:

> *Here is my servant whom I have chosen,*
> *the one I love, in whom I delight;*
> *I will put my Spirit on him,*
> *and he will proclaim justice to the nations.*
> *He will not quarrel or cry out;*
> *no one will hear his voice in the streets.*
> *A bruised reed he will not break,*

and a smouldering wick he will not snuff out,
till he has brought justice through to victory.
In his name the nations will put their hope.

We see glimpses of this same tenderness in David, showing steadfast love and keeping his promises; for example, when he summoned Mephibosheth to his palace.[1]

Entering Jerusalem as king (compare 2 Samuel 6-8 with Matthew 21), Jesus ended up being rejected by the same crowd, and all his 'mighty men' ran away.[2] The kingdom was given to those who would produce its fruit: the stone the builders rejected became the cornerstone (Matthew 21:42-43). But in him the nations will put their hope, people from every tribe, language, people and nation purchased by his blood (Revelation 5:9). Even Israel as a whole will one day look on the one they pierced (Zechariah 12:10).

WHAT MAKES THIS BOOK DIFFERENT FROM OTHERS IN THIS CATEGORY?

First, many books have been written on the life of David, but few are aimed specifically at assisting with leadership development. Yet David went through many tests in his 20s and 30s, and there is much we can glean from his story, and as we will see there is a lot of biblical material about his life and leadership during this period.

Second, some books on Christian leadership and leadership development can end up selecting important principles or themes from Scripture, supporting them with other data, then summarising how these findings can improve our leadership ability or help us better guide others. Less attention is made to the story in its original context. At others times, a verse or passage is taken as a key to understanding

---

1. 2 Samuel 9 and chapter 14 of this book. Also, read or listen to my short monologue and audio book on this called *The King's Table* which is available across dozens of platforms.
2. Compare 2 Samuel 23 with the disciples response to Jesus' suffering and death.

PART ONE: FIGHTER

IN THIS SECTION, we see God's selection and preparation of David. After being anointed and serving faithfully behind the scenes, he is propelled centre stage and experiences a period of great success and popularity. God was with him, and was throughout his reign.

David had to continue to lead, but also follow the Lord. Rumbling behind the scenes was a jealous, violent leader-in-situ to whom he had to report. It was highly dangerous and deeply unfair for David, but he learned to call more deeply on the Lord in his suffering — he learned to fight the fight of faith, whether on the battlefield or in the royal court. God provided in various ways for David's needs.

Here as in other places in David's life we see clear seeds of the gospel, going right back to the Garden of Eden, as well as practical ways in which to draw on his and our Saviour.

> *And I will put enmity between you and the woman, and between your offspring and hers;*
>
> *he will crush your head, and you will strike his heel.*
>
> **Genesis 3:15**

As the story unfolds, we see this truth played out as Satan tried to crush God's people, including leaders whom God appointed and anointed. The enemy is utterly opposed to God's purposes and seeks to destroy all that God has planned, but he is destined for annihilation having been defeated at the cross.[11] God's seed, i.e. Christ[12] whom leaders like David foreshadow, was, and is, destined to prevail.

---

11. Romans 16:20 and Revelation 20:3 and Colossians 2:15.
12. Galatians 3:16.

tall.[13] Think of those in leadership you know or know about – most are taller than average. Leaders like 'the little corporal', Napoleon of France, are the exception. People tend to want to look *up* to a leader. It's human nature.

If you are or aspire to be a leader of some description in God's kingdom, you may not have thought a lot about your looks or your height. But others will consider it. Even mighty prophets of the Lord like Samuel looked at human appearance.

In interview situations people will consider the background, experience and skills of the person being interviewed. What *won't* be part of the interview assessment in many circles, however, is the state of the person's heart. That's the bad news, but also the good news.

Samuel judged the various 'books' on display — Jesse's sons — by their various covers, their outward appearance. Who was Saul's replacement to get them out of their national predicament? Surely someone with the bearing of a king! But Samuel had a problem with his eyesight, revealing a problem in his own heart. We are no different.

A HEAVENLY PATTERN

The youngest son was missing. When the most important person ever to visit their village arrived, young David was absent. As a parent and grandparent I find it hard to fathom why Jesse didn't insist David was present as well. If you knew the President, Vice-President, King, Queen or Prime Minister was coming to *your* city and perhaps to your *house*, would you not ensure your entire family were at home?!

Jesse too had a problem with his vision, stemming from a sinful, human heart. He didn't think someone so young as David mattered; he could look after the sheep. Samuel's and Jesse's flaws highlight our own. God simply *can't* use some people, can he?

Even singing competitions on TV designed to focus on a person's voice and not their looks end up factoring that major aspect in. Attractive and brilliant people are often picked before ugly and

---

13. https://www.inc.com/john-warrillow/the-surprising-role-height-plays-in-your-potential-as-a-leader.html

unattractive singers. The market judges by appearance; looks sell as well as talent.

Yet God's pattern is typically to pick the weak and lowly things, the people we'd never select, to bring about his purposes. He does this to make sure he keeps the glory (1 Cor 1:26-29). It is his to keep. He is in the business of establishing his kingdom, and uses those after his own heart. And the New Testament makes it clear that David was a man after God's own heart, someone who would obey God in everything (Acts 13:22).

THE HEART OF A KING

David was God's ideal leader, the ideal king, but the story points to Jesus, the chosen and final king. He too was from Bethlehem in Judah, and was not impressive in appearance; nor was his resume, his CV, much to speak of. David's descendant was trained in carpentry (Mark 6:3) yet was *the* man after God's own heart.

> *He had no beauty or majesty to attract us to him, nothing in his appearance that we should desire him.*
>
> **Isaiah 53:2**
>
> *As soon as Jesus was baptized, he went up out of the water. At that moment heaven was opened, and he saw the Spirit of God descending like a dove and alighting on him. And a voice from heaven said, "This is my Son, whom I love; with him I am well pleased."*
>
> **Matthew 3:16-17**

As the 'Greater' David, the Spirit came on Jesus in power. And like David he was set above his brothers, his companions, and anointed with the oil of joy (Hebrews 1:9). David's early life points us to the one who would come after him, the Anointed One on whom we can draw. He knows what it is to be brought up in obscurity. He knows what it is to be overlooked, not received by your own, even in your hometown (Luke 24:20-30; John 1:11). Micah 5:2 also tells us that

CHAPTER

2

TEMPORARY AND PERMANENT SOLUTIONS

A MAN I KNEW ended up in jail for soliciting prostitutes. He suffered judgement in being arrested, and great embarrassment as friends found out. But at the same time he was shown grace by God via his distressed wife: she decided to bail him out. He was comforted in the short term but still needed a long term solution to a deeper problem. It was the same with Saul.

We may, like the example I gave above, suffer some form of judgement for sin. However, in his kingdom purposes God graciously not only provides temporary solutions, but also a long term answer for our deepest needs and underlying issues where sin has taken root.

In our next reading, we see God providing for Saul via his chosen one, as young David is summoned to the royal court.

> *Now the Spirit of the Lord had departed from Saul, and an evil spirit from the Lord tormented him.*
>
> *Saul's attendants said to him, "See, an evil spirit from God is tormenting you. Let our lord command his servants here to search for someone who can play the lyre. He will play when the evil spirit from God comes on you, and you will feel better."*

So Saul said to his attendants, "Find someone who plays well and bring him to me."

One of the servants answered, "I have seen a son of Jesse of Bethlehem who knows how to play the lyre. He is a brave man and a warrior. He speaks well and is a fine-looking man. And the Lord is with him."

Then Saul sent messengers to Jesse and said, "Send me your son David, who is with the sheep." So Jesse took a donkey loaded with bread, a skin of wine and a young goat and sent them with his son David to Saul.

David came to Saul and entered his service. Saul liked him very much, and David became one of his armor-bearers. Then Saul sent word to Jesse, saying, "Allow David to remain in my service, for I am pleased with him."

Whenever the spirit from God came on Saul, David would take up his lyre and play. Then relief would come to Saul; he would feel better, and the evil spirit would leave him.

1 Samuel 16:14-23

THE BACKGROUND

The story demonstrates the amazing providence of God in advancing his anointed one to establish a kingdom, right under the nose of a leader he had rejected. A random servant mentions David as they seek to find relief for Saul.

Saul, the people's solution, had failed. Several times it records that 'an evil (or bad) spirit' sent from God tormented him. He was a man under judgment, that's what rebellion brought him; that's what it also brought the people under his poor leadership. Gripped by fear and without God's anointing, Saul's leadership resulted in rash decisions, an impoverished army, and other leaders having to undertake secret sorties to advance the mission in the way God had intended. For instance, Saul's son Jonathan had to sneak out to take a pop at a Philistine garrison comprising 20 soldiers (see 1 Samuel chapter 14).

It's been the same since Eden. We naturally follow in the footsteps of the first man. Like Saul and Adam we rebel by insisting on our own way. But disobeying God's commands only leads to judgement, pain, and into bondage to sin and the evil one. Scripture says, 'The whole world is under the control of the evil one' (Ephesians 2:2; 1 John 5:19). The devil can even get a foothold in the life of believers who rebel (Ephesians 4:27). Rebellion brought bad news for Saul and the people; it will bring bad news for us. Yet God is gracious.

TEMPORARY RELIEF

Despite his rebellion, God granted Saul relief via his chosen one, David. God is good to all and loving towards everything he has made. He causes the sun to rise on the good and the evil. Everyone experiences this provision from the Creator-King, whether they acknowledge it or not. God has not left himself without testimony (Matthew 5:45; Acts 14:17). And like Saul in this scenario, we can accept help or advice from others we trust when troubled or harassed. God may be gracious and provide temporary relief. Like the anointed harp playing with its positive effect on Saul's mind and spirit, good solutions – such as good healthcare and medicine, or kind words or helpful counsel or good music – are all things we can happily receive. God is gracious. We should accept these. In many situations there are solid, short-term solutions that can give us immediate relief.

A PERMANENT SOLUTION

David's harp playing was a God-send, and clear evidence of the Holy Spirit's power on him as God's choice of king. But it was not enough to save Saul from his sin of rebellion. He did not recognise in David the young, anointed king-to-be.

Yet David's ministry was limited, even at its zenith. There would come a day, an era, when the kingdom of God would come in greater power. The ministry of healing and deliverance that began in earnest in

Jesus' ministry is part of God's gracious provision and evidence of his kingdom breaking in until the day of his return in power and glory. In the different accounts of the gospel (Matthew, Mark etc) we see Jesus bringing the kingdom of God in power to people in many ways, e.g. healing from sicknesses and demons, and miraculously providing food. People gratefully received many of the benefits of the kingdom, but it does not mean they entered the kingdom, anymore than Saul gained anything more than a temporary relief in this life. Many were simply in it personal advancement or benefit: when Jesus' teaching got harder, they refused to believe...they walked away (John 6:60-71).

Jesus had a greater kingdom work to do. This is something David could not bring about: a *complete* solution for the sort of trouble Saul was in. It required a far bigger expression of the kingdom of God, brought about one greater than David. And it would take more than music.

David's descendant, the wonderful God-man who was also born in Bethlehem, provided by his death on the cross a more permanent solution for our deepest need: the forgiveness of sins and deliverance from the evil one. In David's gracious and soothing ministry to a rebellious Saul we see another portrait of the stunning gospel of God, and a small picture of the kindness of God in soothing troubled minds with the peace he brings, the fact and experience of being reconciled with God through faith in our Lord Jesus Christ (Romans 5:1).

PRACTICAL RELEVANCE FOR LEADING

First, let's recognise that just as Saul received from David, God can and does provide temporary relief to troubled minds and bodies. Whether through medical or other legitimate means, let us thank God for his gracious provision to heal and support our bodies.

Second, like David, as those anointed in Christ, we simply do not know at times *how* God will bring about the next step in leading us in his kingdom purposes. David was still 'with' or 'tending the sheep' (a phrase mentioned more than once in surrounding passages – 1 Samuel 16:11 & 19) even though he was genuinely anointed to lead, and as we shall later realise had already been taking on lions and bears in protecting those few sheep. Few it seems were aware or remotely bothered about what David was up to. Younger leaders, regardless of how strongly they sense the call and anointing of God in their lives, need to continue to 'tend' to what it is that God called them to in the first instance. It very well may be a more menial or practical task...just as David was looking after 'a few sheep'.

Whatever your stage or age of development as a leader, be assured that the Lord is sovereign and knows when and how much public exposure to allow your way. Those thrust into the limelight at an early age often face trials peculiar to the task, or behind the scenes. For example, in 19th Century England, young Charles Spurgeon, barely 20 years of age, became the toast of London due to his wonderful preaching gift that drew crowds of thousands; many people came to faith. The Lord was clearly with him, but being popular was clearly a trial rather than a blessing to him. And when during a large public gathering he was leading seven people were trampled to death in a stampede (due to a false fire alarm) his mental health took a massive blow. He collapsed on stage and went into seclusion for two weeks. Recording the incident in later years, his wife said he never again preached with as much power. But he faithfully discharged the ministry entrusted to him, seeing thousands come to faith, and 900 men go through his pastors' college. His sermons and books were regularly published around the English-speaking world for up to 25 years after his death.

With the advent of social media over the last 20 years, the opportunities but also the risks involved in being in the public eye should be even more apparent. Exert too much public pressure on a young leader and you can stunt their growth. Denis Clark, at one time the European Director of Youth For Christ, said, "Foster a reputation and it will devour you; forsake it, and it will keep you." Our inward advancement in the things of God is more important than our outward, public appearance. It's a principle which never changes. Character is always more important than charisma or chemistry, and that often involves faithfully getting on with things behind the scenes when no one is looking. Coaches in many fields know this.

Our good deeds find us out eventually, just like any continued sin.

The sins of some are obvious, reaching the place of judgment ahead of them; the sins of others trail behind them. In the same way, good deeds are obvious, and even those that are not obvious cannot remain hidden forever.

1 Timothy 5:24-25

Third, like that servant who tipped off Saul about David, you might end up serving in a role right under the nose of someone in some significant position of earthly power. Other biblical examples are Nehemiah, cupbearer to a king; and Esther, a Jew selected at just the right time in God's purposes to enter the royal court. Whatever our role, we can bring much good to others in serving them.

For those older it might involve our commending a younger person for some practical task. They have what the organisation needs, possess good character, carry themself well in how they talk (and privately you may sense that the Lord's in it too).

It's sometimes those with eyes to see who observe solid character and / or spiritual progress in others serving behind the scenes. Over his career, one mid-level manager in a large organisation was noted for having brought to the attention of senior management a high percentage of people who later went on to occupy significant roles within the organisation. He was like an in-house talent spotter and trainer.

The servant's description of David is also a wonderful depiction of Christ, a son of Bethlehem who demonstrated courage, spoke well, didn't make a noise about it but simply got on with his Father's business. The Lord was, and is, with him! Like that servant let us commend *him* to others when asked and demonstrate His life. He is Christ in us, the hope of glory! (Colossians 1:27)

Fourth, whatever our role, our actions can raise questions as to the source of the power that enables and motivates us, whatever sort of good it is that we are doing, according to the gifts God has given us by his Spirit. By our good deeds and good lives, the gospel becomes attractive to others who watch us (Titus 2:10). When asked, let us point them to the permanent solution found in David's Lord, the Messiah Jesus. His death and resurrection provide eternal relief for our souls, and an invitation to receive a kingdom that will last forever. From that same Saviour we can also receive fresh power from the Holy Spirit to help us keep doing good to others and extending the kingdom of God.

No matter our leadership function, in Christ we can bring much good to people in serving them. This is from God and does not go unnoticed by the Master who created us. Indeed, it is he who set us aside, and it is he who set aside these very types of good works for us to do, long before we ever imagined doing them (Ephesians 2:10). Isn't that incredible and empowering? Christ is before and in all. So let us do the work he has appointed for us.

Service is at the heart of the gospel, so regardless of the grace given us, the type of role in the kingdom to which we've been assigned, let us do it all for the Master and play sweetly for him in the exercise of our gifts and abilities.

QUESTIONS FOR REFLECTION OR DISCUSSION

1. As a developing leader can you thank God for keeping you behind the scenes as part of this stage of your spiritual development?

2. Are you faithfully getting on with what you've been asked to do, drawing on the anointing with power that God gave you by his Spirit for the task that you have at this time?

3. As you develop in your leadership, can you spot younger 'anointed ones' in whom God is at work? If even sinful Saul received the benefit, so can we!

4. Why don't you take a moment to fix your eyes on God's Servant, Jesus, who ministered with power on earth, and ministers now through his body, the Church, dispensing all manner of gifts, both temporary and permanent in the expansion of kingdom?

CHAPTER

3

VICTORY

A s I WROTE in the introduction, this episode highlights some wonderful aspects of how the Lord Jesus has dealt with the scourge of sin and leads us in victory against the enemy. The main point for us is *not* identifying with David as someone with faith, as attractive as that seems. We can actually miss the bigger picture, the wider view, if we zoom in on this and jump straight to applying the biblical text. Of primary importance is where this story fits in as part of God's overall plan of redemption. That God raised up David points us to our Lord and Christ (the Anointed One), the Messiah who was victorious over sin and death by his own sacrificial death on the cross – something that Scripture has been hinting at from the very start. Just as the onlooking soldiers gripped with fear saw David's courageous actions then followed him, so too the Church follows Christ in victory. The soldiers needed someone to deliver and lead them, a new type of leader who could pull them all together in a way none of the judges or deliverers could in times past – one who could usher in a victorious kingdom. Like the soldiers, we need a saviour to lead us. Once we best identify how the story sheds light on the human condition as well as God's grace, we can move more safely to application today.

The reading is 1 Samuel chapter 17. (I've not looked up all the towns and villages for their precise and exact pronunciation, so if anyone knows exactly what they are – I've not taken the time to look it up – you'll forgive me if I Anglicise them a bit).

Now the Philistines gathered their forces for war and assembled at Sokoh in Judah. They pitched camp at Ephes Dammim, between Sokoh and Azekah. Saul and the Israelites assembled and camped in the Valley of Elah and drew up their battle line to meet the Philistines. The Philistines occupied one hill and the Israelites another, with the valley between them.

A champion named Goliath, who was from Gath, came out of the Philistine camp. His height was six cubits and a span (over 9 feet / 3 metres). He had a bronze helmet on his head and wore a coat of scale armor of bronze weighing five thousand shekels (125lbs / 58kg); on his legs he wore bronze greaves, and a bronze javelin was slung on his back. His spear shaft was like a weaver's rod, and its iron point weighed six hundred shekels (15 lbs / 7kg). His shield bearer went ahead of him.

Goliath stood and shouted to the ranks of Israel, "Why do you come out and line up for battle? Am I not a Philistine, and are you not the servants of Saul? Choose a man and have him come down to me. If he is able to fight and kill me, we will become your subjects; but if I overcome him and kill him, you will become our subjects and serve us." Then the Philistine said, "This day I defy the armies of Israel! Give me a man and let us fight each other." On hearing the Philistine's words, Saul and all the Israelites were dismayed and terrified.

Now David was the son of an Ephrathite named Jesse, who was from Bethlehem in Judah. Jesse had eight sons, and in Saul's time he was very old. Jesse's three oldest sons had followed Saul to the war: The firstborn was Eliab; the second, Abinadab; and the third, Shammah. David was the youngest. The three oldest followed Saul, but David went back and forth from Saul to tend his father's sheep at Bethlehem.

For forty days the Philistine came forward every morning and evening and took his stand.

Now Jesse said to his son David, "Take this ephah (36lbs / 16kg) of roasted grain and these ten loaves of bread for your brothers and hurry to their camp. Take along these ten cheeses to the commander of their unit. See how your brothers are and bring back some assurance from them. They are with Saul and all the men of Israel in the Valley of Elah, fighting against the Philistines."

Early in the morning David left the flock in the care of a shepherd, loaded up and set out, as Jesse had directed. He reached the camp as the army was going out to its battle positions, shouting the war cry. Israel and the Philistines were drawing up their lines facing each other. David left his things with the keeper of supplies, ran to the battle lines and asked his brothers how they were. As he was talking with them, Goliath, the Philistine champion from Gath, stepped out from his lines and shouted his usual defiance, and David heard it. Whenever the Israelites saw the man, they all fled from him in great fear.

Now the Israelites had been saying, "Do you see how this man keeps coming out? He comes out to defy Israel. The king will give great wealth to the man who kills him. He will also give him his daughter in marriage and will exempt his family from taxes in Israel."

David asked the men standing near him, "What will be done for the man who kills this Philistine and removes this disgrace from Israel? Who is this uncircumcised Philistine that he should defy the armies of the living God?"

They repeated to him what they had been saying and told him, "This is what will be done for the man who kills him."

When Eliab, David's oldest brother, heard him speaking with the men, he burned with anger at him and asked, "Why have you come down here? And with whom did you leave those few sheep in the wilderness? I know how conceited you are and how wicked your heart is; you came down only to watch the battle."

"Now what have I done?" said David. "Can't I even speak?" He then turned away to someone else and brought up the same matter, and the men answered him as before. What David said was overheard and reported to Saul, and Saul sent for him.

David said to Saul, "Let no one lose heart on account of this Philistine; your servant will go and fight him."

Saul replied, "You are not able to go out against this Philistine and fight him; you are only a young man, and he has been a warrior from his youth."

But David said to Saul, "Your servant has been keeping his father's sheep. When a lion or a bear came and carried off a sheep from the flock, I went after it, struck it and rescued the sheep from its mouth. When it turned on me, I seized it by its hair, struck it and killed it. Your servant has killed both the lion and the bear; this uncircumcised Philistine will be like one of them, because he has defied the armies of the living God. The LORD who rescued me from the paw of the lion and the paw of the bear will rescue me from the hand of this Philistine."

Saul said to David, "Go, and the LORD be with you."

Then Saul dressed David in his own tunic. He put a coat of armor on him and a bronze helmet on his head. David fastened on his sword over the tunic and tried walking around, because he was not used to them.

"I cannot go in these," he said to Saul, "because I am not used to them." So he took them off. Then he took his staff in his hand, chose five smooth stones from the stream, put them in the pouch of his shepherd's bag and, with his sling in his hand, approached the Philistine.

Meanwhile, the Philistine, with his shield bearer in front of him, kept coming closer to David. He looked David over and saw that he was little more than a boy, glowing with health and handsome, and he despised him. He said to David, "Am I a dog, that you come at me with sticks?" And the Philistine cursed David by his gods. "Come here," he said, "and I'll give your flesh to the birds and the wild animals!"

David said to the Philistine, "You come against me with sword and spear and javelin, but I come against you in the name of the LORD Almighty, the God of the armies of Israel, whom you have defied. This day the LORD will deliver you into my hands, and I'll strike you down and cut off your head. This very day I will give the carcasses of the Philistine army to the birds and the wild animals, and the whole world will know that there is a God in Israel. All those gathered here will know that it is not by sword or spear that the LORD saves; for the battle is the LORD's, and he will give all of you into our hands."

As the Philistine moved closer to attack him, David ran quickly toward the battle line to meet him. Reaching into his bag and taking out a stone, he slung it and struck the Philistine on the forehead. The stone sank into his forehead, and he fell facedown on the ground.

So David triumphed over the Philistine with a sling and a stone; without a sword in his hand he struck down the Philistine and killed him.

David ran and stood over him. He took hold of the Philistine's sword and drew it from the sheath. After he killed him, he cut off his head with the sword.

When the Philistines saw that their hero was dead, they turned and ran. Then the men of Israel and Judah surged forward with a shout and pursued the Philistines to the entrance of Gath and to the gates of Ekron. Their dead were strewn along the Shaaraim road to Gath and Ekron. When the Israelites returned from chasing the Philistines, they plundered their camp.

David took the Philistine's head and brought it to Jerusalem; he put the Philistine's weapons in his own tent.

As Saul watched David going out to meet the Philistine, he said to Abner, commander of the army, "Abner, whose son is that young man?"

Abner replied, "As surely as you live, Your Majesty, I don't know."

The king said, "Find out whose son this young man is."

As soon as David returned from killing the Philistine, Abner took him and brought him before Saul, with David still holding the Philistine's head.

"Whose son are you, young man?" Saul asked him.

David said, "I am the son of your servant Jesse of Bethlehem."

1 Samuel chapter 17 (inserts mine)

THE BACKGROUND

The people had actually been here before – too often. In chapter 7 we read that their leader then, Samuel, had told the army *not* to fear the Philistines, their arch enemy, before the day of battle. But we soon read of them hiding away in fear, following their king, Saul, with 'trembling' (1 Samuel 13:7). Even Jonathan, one of the king's sons in the army, had to sneak out to strike the enemy, such was the stifling effect of a senior leadership full of fear (1 Samuel 14:3). We also know that, incredibly, there were on one occasion just two swords in the entire army: one held by Saul, the other by his son, Jonathan. The rest had home-made weapons fashioned from farming equipment (1 Samuel 13:22-23). The Philistines had knocked out all their munitions factories (black-smiths) permitting them only to have equipment relevant to farming sharpened. Talk about having the odds stacked against you.

In an earlier episode King Saul admitted he had become afraid because his troops were starting to desert; he did not deal well with his fear, and in panic offered a sacrifice to God despite knowing it was only for the priest to do such a thing. It was a clear violation of a heavenly command. Which is why the judgment on him was so strict – he lost the kingship (1 Samuel 15).[14]

By the time Goliath had grown up to become the Philistine's main man, the people of Israel and the army were well used to running in the wrong direction. They were impoverished in terms of weapons *and* courage. The Philistines were definitely on top and they knew it. You can imagine some less-than-brave Philistine soldier standing behind Goliath glaring menacingly and smugly at their Israelite opponents, like children standing behind their mother, holding on to her skirt. Such was their confidence in their hero Goliath, supreme warrior among the Philistines, that they put all their bets, their very lives on him winning any one-on-one scrap with the opposition. This was also a common way to settle fights to reduce loss of life on both sides. If you won, the enemy served you, and vice-versa. For a full 40 days the Philistine taunted the fearful army of Israel, in effect yelling twice a day for six weeks, 'Come and have a go if you think you're hard enough!'

It's not often that we get this amount of description about someone in the Bible. When we do, it's for a reason. We need to take note without pressing the details too far. The point is that Goliath was *big, tall and strong*. On their own, a soldier could not defeat him. To get some sense of what they faced I added modern day weights so we can better appreciate the sheer size and weight of the man. The kit of a modern-day NFL footballer is no more than 15 pounds since they need to run.[15] Goliath's military equipment came in at 140; he would stand and fight. If you have two minutes, search 'Gordon Buchanan polar bear' on YouTube where you will find video footage of a 13-foot polar bear trying to get access to him (a BBC camera man) hiding out in a protective see-through pod. Goliath was around the same height but at the most probably half the weight of a polar bear. But humanly speaking there was no way to win, not a chance.

---

14. Many years later, King Uzziah was banned from the temple and lived in a separate house after the Lord afflicted him with leprosy for being unfaithful in entering the temple of the Lord to burn incense, something only priests were allowed to do (2 Chronicles 26).
15. https://www.latimes.com/sports/story/2019-12-22/ask-sam-farmer-how-much-does-nfl-uniform-weigh accessed 2nd June 2021

Interestingly, since the numeral '40' in the Bible denotes testing we have here a period where the army is being tested. No one passes; no one takes on Goliath. At six weeks it's like some sort of nightmare fast for the entire army. But it's not food they were missing, it was faith. Everyone was instead dismayed and filled with fear, stemming from their leader Saul (1 Samuel 17:11 & 24). It was like a cancer eating out the innermost parts of their fighting spirit; in the face of this monster mere human bravery was simply not enough. What could they do against someone this powerful?

Hardened career criminals will rarely admit to being afraid, but the reality is that because they have so many enemies they have to keep looking in fear over their shoulder. Fear spreads like a virus. It can also cause leaders to freeze, run away, or strike out at those on their side who are threatening, or even just plain annoying.

God often commands and encourages people not to be afraid, especially leaders, who have to take the first step. For example, in the Old Testament the army of Israel was commanded not to be afraid, even ordering a clear out of those who were fearful so that they would not discourage the others (Deuteronomy 20). In the New Testament, Jesus urged his followers not to be afraid, even of those who could end their lives, destroy their bodies (Luke 12:4-5).

But King Saul – who had by now lost his ability, the anointing to lead – became so gripped by his *fear* that instead of trying to kill Goliath he later tried to kill the new, young hero of the army, David, a young leader whose *faith* overcame any fear (1 Samuel 18:12 & 29). Note the contrast. Saul kept a fearful, jealous eye on David. Because he was keen to keep hold of his position, he would suppress any up and coming talent that might threaten him.

WHAT IT TELLS US ABOUT THE HUMAN CONDITION

The scale of Goliath underlines for us the utter hopelessness and feebleness of our attempts to overcome sin and the devil. There is such a thing as healthy fear, such as the fear that you might get killed if you drive with your eyes closed, or if you cross the street without looking.

Then there is the fear as in deep respect for someone. But fear can also be sin, and it traps us.[16] It's why the Bible commands so many times to *not* be afraid but instead trust in God, not our own efforts.

You can probably readily recall being in a store or airport with escalators or travelators. They are usually side by side going in the opposite direction. In the same way, fear and faith travel in opposite ways. If you are afraid, you need to get off that escalator and onto the escalator of faith. The whole army of Israel was travelling in the wrong direction. Only David, who was not even a professional soldier, hopped onto the faith escalator travelling the right way. Put another way, it's like asking which voice you are listening to – the voice of fear or the voice of faith? As with a radio you cannot tune into them both at the same time. Genuine faith only comes via Heaven's frequency. Importantly, chapter 17 verse 11 states that Saul and the Israelites became afraid *when they heard the words of the Philistine.*

GOD'S PROVISION THEN AND HOW IT POINTS US TO CHRIST

David also heard Goliath's words. And like the rest he also heard of the reward for the man who beat Goliath: lots of money, tax-free living for the winner's family, and the king's daughter in marriage. Gold, glory, and a girl! Some reward for a young man. David's primary motivation, however, was none of those: it was the removal of the reproach of just how badly Goliath's thunderous and defying challenge reflected on God's honour and how the people were faring.

So incredulous is Saul with David's request that he obliges the young man and allows him to go and fight Goliath. But it seems that he does not quite take it all in, asking later after the victory 'Whose son are you, young man?' For sure, the troops must have pinched themselves when they saw Goliath falling before David grabbed his sword and cut off his head. Yes, he was definitely dead. Fear evaporated and they charged forward as the Philistines ran for their lives. The tables were turned.

---

16. 'Fear of man will prove to be a snare, but whoever trusts in the LORD is kept safe' (Proverbs 29:25)

In much the same way that God provided a series of deliverers or saviours in the preceding centuries (the judges), so now God provided another one with the Spirit who could save them and drive out the enemy – a Victor. And this time he took the form of a shepherd-king.

Faith in a Greater David

As we are trying to make clear in this book, the broad sweep of David's life and his trajectory as an emerging leader points to one of his descendants, Christ, also born in Bethlehem. Just as the soldiers followed when they saw this weak and small lad David winning a magnificent victory over the giant Goliath, so we too follow when we clearly see that a weak Christ actually won a glorious victory over the giant of sin and death by his cross and resurrection. As with David, it was not with sword or spear. It was with a broken body. And as we shall explore later, just as David was eventually installed as King of Judah and then all Israel, so Jesus the Anointed One was eventually installed as King above all Kings by his resurrection. God has made him both Lord and Christ!

> *Therefore let all Israel be assured of this: God has made this Jesus, whom you crucified, both Lord and Messiah.*
>
> **Acts 2:36**
>
> *I have installed my king on Zion, my holy mountain.*
>
> **Psalm 2:6**
>
> *As to his earthly life (Christ) was a descendant of David, and who through the Spirit of holiness was declared with power to be the Son of God by his resurrection from the dead: Jesus Christ our Lord.*
>
> **Romans 1:4**

PRACTICAL RELEVANCE FOR LEADING

The weakness of the leader-in-situ, Saul, and among the people, was fear. The missing ingredient was faith. Faith encouraged and fanned into flame by a leader filled with it. Saul was afraid; David wasn't.

Decisive action based on clear belief or authority makes for great leadership influence. Faith in the revealed will of God makes for great influence. As the leaders go, so do the people. Think of those times when you have done anything significant in God's kingdom, any steps of faith you have taken. What was your conviction, your reasoning based on? Thin air? No! Either a belief in what you were doing was right in God's sight – you didn't need a special word in season – or simply because you knew deep down that you had clear permission from the Lord to move ahead or ask him for certain things. And where does faith come from? Hearing through the word of Christ (Romans 10:17). So, if we hear God speaking to us, let us combine it with faith, and not fail to obey like those who fell in the desert on the way to the promised land, or like Saul and his influence on the other soldiers (Hebrews 3). In the next chapter we'll consider the importance of godly friendships, so helpful for the purposes of mutual encouragement so our hearts do not grow hard when we hear God speaking to us.

A personal illustration

I can clearly recall the time when for several years my wife and I led a group of (college) students connected with our church. We had a house strategically located in the centre of town, and with a large living room, vital for hosting. We saw many young lives wonderfully changed. We both spent and expended ourselves on them, almost as if we were their parents, even though at the time as a married couple with one child, we were not much older than they were.

Behind the scenes it was not easy for us, however. It was like death was at work in us but life was at work in the lives of the students (2 Corinthians 4:12), such was the transformation in their lives. Due to some changes in our circumstances we became very short of money, so we had to put our house up for sale. It was very difficult, but the right thing to do. The towering cost of the mortgage was simply too much. We faced defeat...but we prayed.

Some time later a man who knew us came to our front door offering to help pay our mortgage each month, stating that he believed, "God was in our ministry to students." We were stunned. We did not actually end up taking him up on his offer but we were encouraged to pray further and put our faith in God. In response, the Lord provided at that time £12,000 (around $18,000) over the course of the next 12 months, and from 12 *completely unrelated sources or people*, none of whom we had asked for money, nor had we told them about our financial needs.[17] I have all the information recorded in my journal at the time.

God clearly knew everything and gave us what we needed. As young leaders we learned from practical experience that God is well able to provide what is needed in any given situation, no matter how large. God brought about a great victory for us, we were greatly encouraged, and we were able to keep our house for the remainder of our ministry there. God, the Victor, stepped in, and we followed and continued to serve those God had given us to care for and lead.

> *If God did not spare his own Son, won't he graciously give us all things that we need?*
> **Romans 8:32**

Whatever your sphere or stage of leadership, know that Christ is your Victor. Have faith in him, follow after him. This is the message of David versus Goliath, the slant on the gospel that provides the insight and encouragement we need in our lives and ministries. Christ our leader overcame sin and death. When we, like the fearful Israelite soldiers, appreciate once more his sword of victory coming down on the enemy's head, when we see how in his weakness he gave himself,

---

17. An older wiser man helped me better understand both approaches to finance (asking or not asking) by referring to Nehemiah, who did ask, and Ezra who didn't. Both were godly men, and both in different roles. But both got to Jerusalem. Let the Lord lead you as to the right approach in your circumstances.

then we take courage and follow after him, slaying the enemy along the road.

And with a growing faith in the Victor, your developing leadership will have an even greater effect on those who look to you as an example as you follow Christ.

QUESTIONS FOR REFLECTION OR DISCUSSION

1. Recall or describe a time you or someone else were really afraid (we saw that Goliath's armour is clearly described; fear does not mean denying the scale or details of the difficulty in front of you.)

2. As you've considered the story of David and Goliath again, what new insights have you gleaned about the soldiers' fear and David's victory?

3. What specific thing(s) are you trusting God for at present? It could be related to your home life, work, church, neighbours or some aspect of ministry.

4. As you look to follow the Victor who beckons you to follow after him, how specifically can you continue in faith about this matter?

5. We saw that the Israelite soldiers surged forward when they saw Goliath dead and the Philistines on the run. Using this story, how specifically could you encourage 'another soldier in the ranks' as it were – a fellow believer who may be fearful and needs to trust in Christ the Victor? It could also be a non-believer gripped with fear, and we can point them to Christ the Victor through this wonderful Old Testament story.

CHAPTER

4

FRIENDSHIP

"Make new friends, keep the old
One is silver, the other gold."

Ralph Waldo Emerson

David took the Philistine's head and brought it to Jerusalem; he put the Philistine's weapons in his own tent. As Saul watched David going out to meet the Philistine, he said to Abner, commander of the army, 'Abner, whose son is that young man?'

Abner replied, 'As surely as you live, Your Majesty, I don't know.'

The king said, 'Find out whose son this young man is.'

As soon as David returned from killing the Philistine, Abner took him and brought him before Saul, with David still holding the Philistine's head.

'Whose son are you, young man?' Saul asked him.

David said, 'I am the son of your servant Jesse of Bethlehem.'

After David had finished talking with Saul, Jonathan became one in spirit with David, and he loved him as himself. From that day Saul kept David with him and did not let him return home to his family. And Jonathan made a covenant with David because he loved him as himself. Jonathan took off the robe he was wearing and gave it to David, along with his tunic, and even his sword, his bow and his belt.

1 Samuel 17:54 - 18:4

THE BACKGROUND

Recognising a true peer

WHEN YOUNG DAVID was brought before King Saul after he had beaten Goliath, he identified himself as the 'son of Jesse of Bethlehem'. The episode marks the end of a long section in 1 Samuel which began at the start of chapter 16 where the same phrase is used. Still in his hands was Goliath's bloody head.

Perhaps Jonathan was in on this remarkable conversation – the text doesn't tell us – for in the next sentence it is recorded for us that, 'After David had finished talking with Saul, Jonathan became one in spirit with David.'

Either way, a young lad not yet possessing the physical stature of a grown man had just accomplished what no soldier in the entire army had managed to do, including the commander Abner, *and* Jonathan himself despite having led an earlier successful sortie. David defeated the giant man with the giant mouth and the giant spear. And he did it without a sword of his own. He took Goliath's head into Jerusalem. In what would later become the capital city – the City of David – the young shepherd boy walked right through the gates of a city still occupied by the Jebusites, with the giant head of the fighter no one dared to go up against.

Quite how Saul did not recognise David is not clear; the text doesn't tell us. Perhaps it was disbelief. Perhaps with all the comings and goings of the royal court he could not quite remember. We also remember that Saul was being tormented in spirit – hardly conducive to an accurate recollection of events (a parallel might be being under the influence of drugs).

Any feelings of sheepishness on the part of the watching troops would have been quickly superseded by the smell of victory wafting across to their side of the valley where the face-off had been every day for six weeks. The giant was at last slain! Jonathan, one of Saul's sons, would have found it very difficult to take his eyes off young David when he got to see and hear him up close. Here was a kindred spirit, a young man not given to being afraid of men but instead putting his faith in God and going head-to-head with the opposition.

Despite his earlier heroics in taking out 20 enemy soldiers in one of their forward operating bases (1 Samuel 14:14), it seems Jonathan too had insufficient courage, skill, or most importantly sufficient faith to face Goliath. His father the king and commander-in-chief displayed weak leadership that did not bolster the men to believe God; his actions had only enhanced their fears. Such was the spiritual and military malaise at the time that Jonathan had to creep out from camp unnoticed so he could undertake a mission. Jonathan knew the sweet taste of personal victory in trusting God and stepping out in faith just with his armour bearer. He also appreciated the resultant impact on other soldiers around him gripped with fear (some had been hiding in the hills). God had sent a panic among the enemy, and the other soldiers took courage and advanced, and God saved Israel that day. We can read about this in 1 Samuel chapter 14.

Now for perhaps the first time Jonathan was looking at a peer: young David, a true contemporary, someone prepared to lead by example by facing seemingly impossible odds. Someone who clearly knew all about going forward, fighting; someone with faith.

HOW DID JONATHAN RESPOND?

Jonathan and David became best mates, buddies, pals. Despite being heir to the throne, Jonathan conceded that David would become king one day instead of him. Jonathan had been there from the start, at that initial and crucial conversation, handing David his robe, armour, sword, belt, and bow, and made a promise to him.

The word for 'robe' at that time would often have denoted a royal robe. If Israel followed the same customs in this matter as other nations (let's not forget that the people wanted a king just like the other nations around them – 1 Samuel 8) then as crown prince, Jonathan was effectively renouncing his claim to the throne.[18]

Twice it says of Jonathan that, 'he loved him [David] as himself.' Theirs was a deep bond in spirit, not spirit and body – that's reserved for a man and his wife.

Athletes and especially soldiers thrown together in competitive games and particularly military combat understand this unique bond. David and Jonathan were one in spirit about the mission they shared: serving the God of Israel in battle and conquering the invading Philistines. They were not unlike spiritual twins who discovered each other later as young adults.

We see further evidence of this in later encounters; for example, when David was on the run from Saul, Jonathan said to him, 'Whatever you want me to do, I'll do for you' (1 Samuel 20:4). And in this same moment in what they both realised could have been their last ever time talking together, Jonathan had declared:

> *"May the LORD be with you as he has been with my father. But show me unfailing kindness like the LORD's kindness as long as I live, so that I may not be killed, and do not ever cut off your kindness from my family—not even when the LORD has cut off every one of David's enemies from the face of the earth". So Jonathan made a covenant with the house of David, saying, "May the LORD call David's enemies to account." And Jonathan had David reaffirm his oath out of love for him, because he loved him as he loved himself."*
>
> **1 Samuel 20:13-17**

Jonathan knew deep down that David was the true anointed one destined to replace his father and see the kingdom extended, just as God had promised long ago to Abraham (Genesis 15:18-21).

But they did meet one more time, when David was in hiding.

---

18. See *IVP Bible Background Commentary* by Walton, Matthews and Chavalas.

David stayed in the wilderness strongholds and in the hills of the Desert of Ziph. Day after day Saul searched for him, but God did not give David into his hands.

While David was at Horesh in the Desert of Ziph, he learned that Saul had come out to take his life. And Saul's son Jonathan went to David at Horesh and helped him find strength in God. "Don't be afraid," he said. "My father Saul will not lay a hand on you. You will be king over Israel, and I will be second to you. Even my father Saul knows this." The two of them made a covenant before the LORD. Then Jonathan went home, but David remained at Horesh.

1 Samuel 23:14-18

Note the risk Jonathan takes in supporting David's cause. It was completely against his father's wishes and put his own life at risk.

HOW GRACE WAS EXHIBITED THEN AND HOW IT POINTS US TO CHRIST NOW

We can look at this in several ways for our encouragement. First, God provided for David a true friend, a close brother, and at a time when David would soon come under intense pressure. From the very beginning of his dramatic entrance into the fray – in a sense the start of his public ministry, at least for a season – Jonathan was there for David.

Second, we see in David's stunning victory over Goliath that saved Israel a fantastic image of Christ's ministry, and victory over death. Like David he went up against a champion no one could defeat, one that had always won, one that stung. Death was put to death, not by the sword but by the death of Christ. In that sense he decapitated it: he took off its head. The Scripture says elsewhere, 'There was no way for death to hold him' (Acts 2:24); he broke 'the power of him who holds the power of death—that is, the devil' by his death on the cross (Hebrews 2:14). He now holds in his hands the keys of death (Revelation 1:18).

Paul the apostle later wrote:

Where, O death, is your victory?
Where, O death, is your sting?

1 Corinthians 15:55

And just as the Philistines were still active afterwards, the battle isn't over. Yet the champion (death) and him who holds it, has been crushed. And while, as the Scripture says, 'your body is subject to death because of sin, the Spirit gives life because of righteousness' (Romans 8:10). Christ's death and the aftermath of his victory, including empowering his followers with his Spirit, provides us with eternal life. His death means reconciliation. So we boast about him.

Scripture says:

For if, while we were God's enemies, we were reconciled to him through the death of his Son, how much more, having been reconciled, shall we be saved through his life! [11] *Not only is this so, but we also boast in God through our Lord Jesus Christ, through whom we have now received reconciliation.*

Romans 8:10-11

His resurrection, ascension, and continuing intercession for us also shows the great love of Christ for us who were once his enemies.

It says:

Christ Jesus who died—more than that, who was raised to life—is at the right hand of God and is also interceding for us. Who shall separate us from the love of Christ?

Romans 8:34-35

Third, in those additional sections we read or have listened to, we also see foreshadowed by Jonathan's actions the behaviour of individual believers and the true church as a whole: surrendering, putting Christ first as they see who he really is.

Can you see the parallel?

As I am trying to make clear in this book, the Bible is about

Christ, the story should lead us to him. The New Testament is filled with examples of people and whole groups of people laying down their lives and possessions for the Lord Jesus. That's what affection for God's servant Jesus does to the true believer, just as Jonathan showed affection for God's servant David.

A cricketer

Englishman C.T. Studd (1860-1931) was a famous cricket player who later served the Lord in China and India. In his early 50s he then set off for the centre of Africa to preach the gospel and make disciples, despite the advice of his doctor (he'd already suffered from various diseases he'd caught during his travels).

A note was found on his desk after he left:

> *If Jesus Christ is God and died for me, then no sacrifice can be too great for me to make for him.*

Like Jonathan, Studd took risks in his support of Christ's cause, to see him honoured as king among people far away who did not know him. Studd's little book 'The Chocolate Soldier'[19] is well worth a read, especially if you are struggling with being passive, not taking any initiative in things, not partnering with God in His mission.

Fourth, through the effect of David's actions we see brotherhood, family develop. Through the new covenant – the Lord's steadfast love shown by the shedding of Christ's blood for us – Jesus becomes an elder brother to us, and is not ashamed to call us his brothers (Hebrews 2:11). He is that faithful friend like no other.

PRACTICAL RELEVANCE FOR LEADING

Connecting after an event

Perhaps you have felt such a moment, of being joined in spirit to someone through some shared event or occasion, someone who for you

---

19. 'The Chocolate Soldier, or Heroism–the Lost Chord of Christianity' available on several platforms.

was perhaps the first person you can relate to deeply as a genuine peer, whatever your context and particular stage of leadership development. Perhaps the other man demonstrated clear courage and leadership to go for something. If you've felt that bond, then don't waste the moment; like Jonathan, build on it. You may not feel compelled to give them some personal stuff like Jonathan did, but you can quickly build on the connectedness somehow and see if they return the feeling. It could end up lasting a long time. Such a friendship could also end up saving your life or your career, as it did with David.

A young man in training for church leadership lost his temper one day with another trainee and was about to punch him. A friend grabbed hold of his arm as he drew it back to strike the other man in anger. It probably helped save him from wrecking his ministry potential, at least in the short- to mid-term, for what church would take on a young leader who hits people if they provoke him? His friend loved him enough to step in and stop him from doing something reckless.

I remember connecting with another guy, Brad, when we were both playing football (soccer) when I went into training for leadership. The fact that I was Scottish and he was American was a sweet, added dimension to the relationship. Brad and I were soon able to talk about all sorts of stuff we were learning, other leaders, our growing convictions, and how we were getting on at home with our young wives. It wasn't the stuff of life and death but it certainly involved working through some painful times and enjoying the joyful ones. Despite now being thousands of miles apart, many times over the years we have talked frankly by email, 'phone or video about work situations, hard leadership decisions, and battles within ourselves. When we meet up every few years it's like it was yesterday.

Such bonds are only formed when you are on some sort of journey together, and especially when you are under some sort of pressure; the more acute, the deeper the bond.

Patrick Bury, a former British Army Captain reflecting on his time during war, writes:

People have tried to take our lives and together we have taken life. I feel traces of it now, but later I will realise there is a bond, an unspoken, intangible magnetic bind that holds us together and apart from civilians. Of shared experiences, shared tests, of danger and death, which no one else can understand or even wants to. A closeness that is rarely equalled outside these circles. A mutual understanding, an affirmation of manhood.[20]

Qualities and questions

You can't follow, lead or be mates with someone you don't respect. You respect them because of some action they took or appreciate something about their character or beliefs they acted on. From what we've read we know that for Jonathan it was because of David's bravery and faith in the Lord. For David, it was Jonathan's willingness to give up his kit, his right to the throne and make David promise that he would look after his descendants once he took the throne.

Here are three things from this you might want to look for in someone, or demonstrate yourself, if you are to develop lasting bonds of friendship.

1. *Bravery.* David squared up to Goliath. Have you or the other person faced up to something more powerful or someone far bigger than themselves or that your church or organisation is facing? Have you or they taken a clear step of faith over some matter despite tough circumstances, and then seen the hand of God rewarding that faith?

2. *Loyalty.* Later on Jonathan helped David escape Saul who was out to kill him. Does the person help and encourage others when it really matters? Do *you* stick with others?

3. *Sacrifice.* David recognised Jonathan was giving up a huge amount by giving him his sword etc. There were very few decent weapons around at the time. It was also symbolic. Jonathan in effect was saying, 'You're the one to lead out first, not me.' So has the person

---

20. *Call Sign Hades*, Patrick Bury, Simon and Schuster, London, UK, 2010, p 258-259

done something that really cost them? It may be for someone else, or it may have been for you.

A spouse

What about those reading this who are unmarried and want a wife? Husbands are to lay down their lives for their wives (Ephesians 5:25). If you are serious about a girl, then your love for her should begin to involve elements of sacrifice that draw her admiration as well as exhibiting Christ. You can obviously do that more when you're married, but demonstrating that pattern of behaviour is a godly thing. That's the whole point of headship: 100% love on the part of the man, which inspires confidence in her that you are someone to partner with and follow in the journey.

A spouse can be not only a best friend but like a life-saver with sound advice. Many a man has been saved from doing something stupid by listening to some sensible advice from his wife (I can certainly testify to that). Winston Churchill, leader of the UK during World War II, once ignored some sensible advice from his wife, Clementine. After the war she was reading his first campaign speech to get re-elected. She advised him not to compare the main opposition party's policy to the cruel war-time German police, the Gestapo. He ignored her and it backfired. Other members of the Parliament were certainly not impressed. He was not re-elected after the war was over. But once you've said it you've said it. You know what I'm talking about. Social media makes it even more imperative we choose our words carefully...or say nothing. People listen very carefully to what leaders say. So if you find someone good to marry, don't lose them. For many a man this may include a wife who is willing to help her man not 'put his foot in it'. In the same way, a woman in a prominent leadership role will find encouragement in a husband who supports her to the hilt behind the scenes; for example, the first female Prime Minister of the U.K., Margaret Thatcher, said her husband, Dennis, was a rock.

From older to younger

To those of you reading or listening to this who are older, I would encourage you not to hold back in pursuing friendships with those younger or less experienced in leadership than yourself. Don't wait for them to come to you. Some find it intimidating approaching older, respected figures. Consider many leaders in the Bible and the less experienced leaders they helped develop, and recall who took the initiative. If you need help with this, do please read my book *Mentoring Ministry: How God Can Use You to Shape the Following Generations*[21] It's available in e-book and paperback formats, but also free as an audiobook on some platforms.

I recently contacted some younger men I had the privilege of investing in many years ago when they were between 16 and 22 years of age. Now older they live many miles away from me, and my role in their lives is occasional, more two-way, but the friendship remains. It is no different than when children grow up (my children are now adults). Respect remains, as does the warmth, forged through prior experiences at a formative time in their development that you happen to have had some important input into.

John Newton of 'Amazing Grace'

You never know who you might have in your hands for a while. Former British slave trader John Newton, who wrote the song 'Amazing Grace', was instrumental in encouraging young William Wilberforce, then in his mid-20s, to commit to serving as a politician and not go into full-time work as a church leader as some expected. Not long after their first meeting, Newton wrote to Wilberforce, saying:

> *'Our time together quite freed me from reserve and awkwardness that I feel in the company of some persons who I greatly love and honour… I seem nowhere more at home or more disposed to think aloud, that is to speak without restraint or premeditation, than when I am with you.'*

---

21. Available as an e-book, paperback, and also as a free audiobook on some platforms to serve those around the world with perhaps no credit / bank card.

In other words, Newton felt a freedom in his conversation, a connection with Wilberforce that he didn't feel so much with others. Newton got on really well with young Wilberforce and could see where his talents might be best deployed. The consequences of that warm and open relationship had far reaching consequences for thousands of Africans then being enslaved by British and other traders. In his role as a politician, Wilberforce ended up campaigning against slavery for 40 years, leading to its ban across most of the British Empire.

Newton was also a friend to other pastors, being a massive encouragement to them through regular pastors' gatherings. And like David, Newton also knew about the love of a woman; at times he felt so close to his wife, Polly, that he feared he was idolising her.[22]

I've been fortunate enough to develop deep friendships with a few men who have become very dear to me. I also have a wonderful wife and soulmate.

Look out for those you seem to connect with. Ask God for those kindred spirits who you can spar in life with. Perhaps like Jonathan you just need to look up and see who is actually competing well in the race of faith. Or like David perhaps you need to be willing to receive the encouragement of someone who has approached you. Don't dismiss it. Such relationships are incredibly precious. So, seek friendship with solid contemporaries in your sphere of work or ministry; make good friends among other men that God sends you.

DIVINE FRIENDSHIP

Jonathan and David had a wonderful bond. A covenant. Do you know the love of Christ personally? He has made a new covenant in his blood shed for you. Near the end of their journey together Jesus said to his closest followers that they were now his friends, not simply servants (John 15:15). One of them, John, seemed especially close to Jesus at points. During the last supper he is seen leaning back against Jesus' chest as all the men would have laid sideways around the dinner table

---

22. See *John Newton: From Disgrace to Amazing Grace*, Crossway, UK, 2013. By Jonathan Aitken and Philip Yancey

(John 13:23). We should not think it strange that God loves to draw people close to him. And for that was needed a covenant to bridge the gap between God and man: the cross. It is sometimes during people's most difficult hours that they sense the presence of God most acutely.

The Song of Songs underlines not only the importance of marital love, but in *general* terms it speaks of the affection between Christ and his bride; it's a personal relationship, not something distant between a Master and a slave.

Song writer Martin Smith of the band *Delirious* wrote these words:

What a friend I've found
Closer than a brother
I have felt Your touch
More intimate than lovers

Jesus, Jesus, Jesus
Friend forever

What a hope I've found
More faithful than a mother
It would break my heart
To ever lose each other.[23]

If you are in Christ, you can be sure of the faithful and steadfast friendship of the Lord, expressed supremely in his death on the cross. It is his heroic and sacrificial act that means God can be a friend and no longer an enemy (Romans 5:1-11). Moreover, that same God can also bring faithful friends as well as a spouse into our lives. Isn't that amazing?

---

23. Martin Smith, 1998. Curious? Music UK/PRS. The song is administered in the US and Canada by EMI CMG Publishing.

QUESTIONS FOR REFLECTION OR DISCUSSION

1. Do you personally know this covenant love of the Lord for you – his death that makes friendship with God possible?

2. Who do you have a close bond with, or did have at one time? What is it about them that you admire or that you admired?

3. Do you have any peers who have shown bravery, loyalty or sacrifice whom you could befriend?

4. Do you need to ask God specifically for someone who is like a more experienced boxer to spar with and 'fight the fight of faith', or perhaps someone older who is like a trainer or coach, someone who has gone many rounds in the ring? Who could you approach?

5. If you're an older man or an older leader, who are the younger leaders you could develop? Why not take the initiative? In Scripture, older or more experienced leaders nearly always invited younger or less experienced leaders into relationship and ministry.

6. Do you need to ask God for a marriage partner to share your life, heart and faith with? A kindred spirit who also loves the Lord may be a great match – if they feel the same way about you!

CHAPTER

5

OPPOSITION

Consider him who endured such opposition from sinners.
Hebrews 12:2

O UR NEXT EPISODE begins at verse 5 and ends at verse 30 of chapter 18. We are given a clear picture of David's growing success as an officer in the army. At the start, everyone in the military was pleased with him; by the end, his name was well known.

You might wonder why it says this since he was the one that killed Goliath. Didn't everyone know his name by then? Perhaps one reason is that he had not proven himself as a commander of a unit of men. As immense as the victory over Goliath was, David had been a mere lad. Was it an amazing one-off victory or could he lead a group of fighting men? This episode tells us that it is clear to everyone in the army that he could lead a large group of them into battle and crush the enemy... every time. But not everyone was happy.

(Those of you listening to this who speak Hebrew...you'll forgive me I use a mix of Anglicised and Hebrew-sounding expressions of names particularly.)

Whatever mission Saul sent him on, David was so successful that Saul gave him a high rank in the army. This pleased all the troops, and Saul's officers as well.

When the men were returning home after David had killed the Philistine, the women came out from all the towns of Israel to meet King Saul with singing and dancing, with joyful songs and with timbrels and lyres. As they danced, they sang:

"Saul has slain his thousands,
and David his tens of thousands."

Saul was very angry; this refrain displeased him greatly. "They have credited David with tens of thousands," he thought, "but me with only thousands. What more can he get but the kingdom?" And from that time on Saul kept a close eye on David.

The next day an evil spirit from God came forcefully on Saul. He was prophesying in his house, while David was playing the lyre, as he usually did. Saul had a spear in his hand and he hurled it, saying to himself, "I'll pin David to the wall." But David eluded him twice.

Saul was afraid of David, because the LORD was with David but had departed from Saul. So he sent David away from him and gave him command over a thousand men, and David led the troops in their campaigns. In everything he did he had great success, because the LORD was with him. When Saul saw how successful he was, he was afraid of him. But all Israel and Judah loved David, because he led them in their campaigns.

Saul said to David, "Here is my older daughter Merab. I will give her to you in marriage; only serve me bravely and fight the battles of the LORD." For Saul said to himself, "I will not raise a hand against him. Let the Philistines do that!"

But David said to Saul, "Who am I, and what is my family or my clan in Israel, that I should become the king's son-in-law?" So when the time came for Merab, Saul's daughter, to be given to David, she was given in marriage to Adriel of Meholah.

Now Saul's daughter Michal was in love with David, and when they told Saul about it, he was pleased. "I will give her to him," he thought, "so that she may be a snare to him and so that the hand of the Philistines may be against him." So Saul said to David, "Now you have a second opportunity to become my son-in-law."

Then Saul ordered his attendants: "Speak to David privately and say, 'Look, the king likes you, and his attendants all love you; now become his son-in-law.'"

They repeated these words to David. But David said, "Do you think it is a small matter to become the king's son-in-law? I'm only a poor man and little known."

When Saul's servants told him what David had said, Saul replied, "Say to David, 'The king wants no other price for the bride than a hundred Philistine foreskins, to take revenge on his enemies.'" Saul's plan was to have David fall by the hands of the Philistines.

When the attendants told David these things, he was pleased to become the king's son-in-law. So before the allotted time elapsed, David took his men with him and went out and killed two hundred Philistines and brought back their foreskins. They counted out the full number to the king so that David might become the king's son-in-law. Then Saul gave him his daughter Michal in marriage.

When Saul realized that the LORD was with David and that his daughter Michal loved David, Saul became still more afraid of him, and he remained his enemy the rest of his days.

The Philistine commanders continued to go out to battle, and as often as they did, David met with more success than the rest of Saul's officers, and his name became well known.

1 Samuel 18:5-30

BACKGROUND, CONTEXT, AND SAUL'S RESPONSE

The Hebrew word for *success* appears four times. The text supplies the reason: *the Lord was with David,* or *with him,* a phrase we see three times. Moreover, David is *loved* by every person or group of people named in the story: Saul's daughter Michal, the whole country, even the royal court attendants – if we are to believe Saul. But not Saul himself. The one who used to *love* David greatly (the same word for love used in chapter 16:21) now finds him a huge threat. How ironic. At root Saul is *afraid* – a word mentioned three times – and each time it is directly connected to the fact that the Lord was *with* David. We've seen this dynamic before. It takes us right back to Bethlehem when Samuel turned up with his horn of oil to anoint young David.

> *Then Samuel took the horn of oil and anointed him in the midst of his brothers. And the Spirit of the LORD rushed upon David from that day forward. And Samuel rose up and went to Ramah. Now the Spirit of the LORD departed from Saul, and a harmful spirit from the LORD tormented him.*

1 Samuel 16:13-14

We are now seeing the outworking of the impact of the work of the Holy Spirit upon David in contrast to an entirely different spirit oppressing Saul. Saul had rebelled and God was 'sorry' that he had appointed him king (1 Samuel 15:35), the same word used in the original in Genesis 6:6 in respect of God's 'regret' over creating mankind. Saul's rebellion was like the sin of witchcraft. Almost as a further sign of God's displeasure, Samuel the prophet, who had led Israel before Saul and anointed him as king, never visited Saul again. God was clearly with David, but against Saul.

Outside the royal court, people at the time would not have been aware of Saul's issues. But we get to see behind the curtain. It's the same today. For instance, a businessman or preacher or elder may come across really well in public, but behind the scenes could be treating people really badly. But it won't go on forever. A good Old Testament example is Samson, who was still endued with power after entering a prostitute's house. But in time he loses his ability to lead, at one point early on not realising that the Lord had left him (Judges 16:1-20).

So at the human level we observe a man greatly threatened upon hearing *that* song about David's tens of thousands and Saul's thousands. It was simply too much. He thought his position was under threat, so kept an eye on David. But the very next day the spiritual consequences of his rebellion, and God's judgment upon him as a result, were further played out. His own sin and the oppression of the enemy led Saul to seek to kill David. Two murder attempts. When you stop and think about it, it's pretty shocking.

David saw first-hand the consequences of losing your anointing as king, even if you hold on to your position. Not having the Lord with you carries massive consequences. While not connected with this episode in David's life, many years later David wrote 'Take not your Holy Spirit from me' in his prayer of confession after taking Bathsheba as his wife and killing off her husband, Uriah (Psalm 51:11). He had seen for himself before the terrible consequences of the Lord leaving you – he did not want that happening to him.

Disobedience leads to God's judgment and oppression, and for Saul fear ensued followed by further sin and rebellion.

So how would God's wonderful purpose prevail? How would the anointed one, David, ascend to the throne when things looked so bleak? How would the man after God's own heart, God's choice of king, succeed and see the kingdom established? How would God's covenant promise to Abraham that his descendants would possess the land all the way from the Euphrates River far to the north down to the Wadi of Egypt in the south be fulfilled? (Genesis 15:18-21). A leader was needed, one who would bring the nation together and defeat their main enemy (the Philistines) who had taken up residence in large tracts of their land. Saul wasn't the one.

Saul then removed David from what was essentially a role back at

HQ and out into the field of battle commanding a large unit of men (the Hebrew for the word a 'thousand' can mean a large unit or size). But it doesn't make any difference *where* exactly David is. Saul's fear might cause him to drive David away, but the Lord remains with David wherever he is dispatched.

In keeping with Saul's promise that the man who killed Goliath would be provided one of his daughters in marriage, Merab is given (1 Samuel 17:25). Saul realises that he can use the occasion to expose David to danger on the front ranks in battle. (Interesting when you think about what happened later: David used the same strategy to have Uriah killed.)

We are not told why David declines, except that he does not think he is worthy to be counted the king's son-in-law. So Saul tries to kill him again using another of his daughters, Michal, as a trap. It's ironic that Saul was *pleased* when he learned that Michal had fallen in love with David, for he had certainly *not* been pleased that the Lord was *with* David. Setting him the challenging task of killing a hundred Philistine soldiers, and proving it, he hoped to see him killed on the next sortie. David, not one for doing the minimum required, doubled the foreskin count: a kill count of two hundred men, with the full number counted out before the king. One, two, three…ninety-nine…a hundred and fifty…two hundred. Perhaps Saul was hoping he would be one or two short. I wonder what his face was like when the full number was reached. The one prized by the people is now given the prize of a wife. For Michal too, David is quite a catch, and we see later in Scripture that she is of course keen to protect him, just as Jonathan her brother is.

GOD'S GRACE THEN AND HOW IT POINTS US TO CHRIST

First, in the love and protection shown to David by Michal his wife, respect from the army, and love from the people in general we see the kindness and favour of God. The Lord does not abandon his servants. He has promised never to leave us or forsake us (Matthew 28:19 and Hebrews 13:5). This may often take the form of the support of people who genuinely care about our welfare, and God's will for us. In more difficult situations it may involve offering us protection from those opposed to us.

Second, the contrast between Saul and David shows us the difference between those who, like Saul, operate according to the flesh (that is, according to their sinful nature), and those like David, the promised one on whom the Spirit rested. The one born of the flesh opposes the one born of the Spirit. Paul outlines this principle for us in Galatians 4:29 where he contrasts Isaac (the child born of a promise) and Ishmael (the one born according to the flesh). One is free, the other enslaved; one a child of promise, the other disinherited. Young Isaac was mocked by his older brother, Ishmael, when he was weaned (Genesis 21:1-10). So too those born of the flesh (and not of the Spirit) mock and persecute those born of the Spirit. That verse in Galatians 4:29 says:

> *At that time, the son born according to the flesh persecuted the son born by the power of the Spirit. It is the same now.*

In appealing to the Galatians *not* to go back to a false gospel of works and laws and rules to justify themselves before God, Paul exposes the true nature of legalism and legalists. Such enemies of the gospel, operating out of the flesh, are often bound by weak and pointless and miserable religious rituals or rules that can never bring us to God (Galatians 4). They often strongly oppose the gospel of grace and its messengers.

Even sincere believers can end up succumbing to the belief that their rules or traditions are sacred, going on to oppose those operating more from the principle of spiritual freedom. Sadly, some of us can become so attached to our way of doing things that we can end up missing the point. We are born free in the Spirit and are not to be bound by unnecessary rules and traditions; we are to adapt the means to suit the end, adopting and adapting practices which are in line with biblical principles but which remain culturally relevant.

I once visited a church which was by all accounts culturally stuck in the 1950s. You could have put the entire elderly congregation in a time-machine and taken them back six decades and they would have fitted in perfectly. Tragic. I preached to that effect, but my words fell on deaf ears. I learned later that day that the church had begun some 30 years earlier as a result of a disagreement…over the choice of hymnbook. The church had been built largely on one small tradition.

Think of what Paul was like before he was born of the Spirit – he hunted believers down. It is often those who are very religious or possess a form of godliness but deny the power of God (1 Tim 3:5), and especially those who occupy religious positions, who persecute those born of the Spirit, the true children of God born of a promise. Who was it that put Jesus to death? The religious people (not true religion) and their leaders. More on that in a moment.

As mentioned before, this takes us right back to the garden of Eden:

> *And I will put enmity*
>   *between you and the woman,*
>   *and between your offspring and hers;*
> *he will crush your head,*
>   *and you will strike his heel.*

Genesis 3:15

It is about more than Saul's fear of David; more than about one nation, the Philistines, warring against another, Israel. Behind such actions there lies a cosmic battle: the kingdom of God is sure to advance through the promised offspring, the seed of Abraham, one through whom all nations would be blessed.[24] God raised up David and anointed him. But the enemy the devil will do all he can to oppose God's people and plans.

Another example in the national context is when David was finally anointed king over all Israel many years later – the Philistines came up in full force in search of him (2 Samuel 5:17). Which is why those who are given an anointing to lead may very soon face opposition.

---

24. The promises were spoken to Abraham and to his seed. Scripture does not say "and to seeds," meaning many people, but "and to your seed," meaning one person, who is Christ. Galatians 3:16.

Third, in David we see a man pursued. He is not a fugitive yet, but Saul is most certainly his enemy. He is in as much danger in the royal court as he would be later on after he had made good his escape. As one who prefigures Jesus, we can view this episode and others like it as pointing to 'him who endured such opposition from sinners' (Hebrews 12:3). For example, when Jesus the Anointed One (i.e. the Messiah, the Christ) raised Lazarus from the dead, the chief priests and the Pharisees were greatly threatened. It says:

> ...*the chief priests and the Pharisees called a meeting of the Sanhedrin.*
>
> *"What are we accomplishing?" they asked. "Here is this man performing many signs. If we let him go on like this, everyone will believe in him, and then the Romans will come and take away both our temple and our nation."*
>
> *Meanwhile a large crowd of Jews found out that Jesus was there [Bethany] and came, not only because of him but also to see Lazarus, whom he had raised from the dead. So the chief priests made plans to kill Lazarus as well, for on account of him many of the Jews were going over to Jesus and believing in him.*
>
> **John 11:47-48 and 12:9-11**

They saw Jesus' presence and ministry as something that was going to lead to their demise (compare Saul's 'What more can he get but the kingdom?' with the Pharisees' statement 'The Romans will come and take away both our temple and our nation'). So they made definite plans to kill him...and Lazarus. Again, shocking when you stop and think about it. Not only do they plan to kill Jesus, they plot to put to death a man brought back from death: put him back in the grave. Can you imagine? Utterly opposed to the 'author of life' (Acts 3:15). This whole dynamic underlines that it's a spiritual thing. We wrestle not against flesh and blood, but against powers and principalities (Ephesians 6:12).

As with King Saul, the chief priests and Pharisees were part of the religious establishment, the set up. But God was not with them simply because they held a position. Another example is where Paul (a Jew who believed that the Messiah was Jesus) ended up being persecuted by his fellow Jews. At one point more than forty of them bound themselves with an oath not to eat or drink until they had killed him (Acts 23).

Ultimately, we see the outcome of such opposition in the death of our Lord Jesus. Such great hatred and mocking during his trial and as he hung on the cross, and with all his disciples hiding and the women watching from a distance. Jesus…mocked on the cross as he suffered in agony for our sins and theirs. And yet, 'for the joy set before him he endured the cross, scorning its shame' (Hebrews 12:2). He resisted great opposition and stayed on the cross when he could have easily come down by calling on his Father to rescue him and send a legion of angels.[25]

God fulfilled his promise to install one of David's sons as king. Forever. Christ completed the race as the pioneer, shed his blood for you and me, and sat down at the right hand of the Father (Hebrews 12:2-4).

PRACTICAL RELEVANCE FOR LEADING

1. Let us take to heart the broader picture. The one born of the flesh will be opposed to the one born of the Spirit. If you are called by God and the hand of the Lord is on you, you will face opposition, ultimately from the arch enemy, Satan. The servant is not above the Master. Scripture says:

   If the world hates you, keep in mind that it hated me first. If you belonged to the world, it would love you as its own. As it is, you do not belong to the world, but I have chosen you out of the world. That is why the world hates you. Remember what I told you: 'A servant is not greater than his master.' If they persecuted me, they will persecute you also. If they obeyed my teaching, they will obey yours also.

---

25. "Do you think I cannot call on my Father, and he will at once put at my disposal more than twelve legions of angels? But how then would the Scriptures be fulfilled that say it must happen in this way?" (Matthew 26:53-43).

| **John 15:18-20**

2. As we've seen, during times when we are being opposed for serving the kingdom, God can provide us with others for our comfort and protection; for example, godly friends and acquaintances.

   A fellow pastor once shared with me about the time he was traveling in China and got arrested for attending an underground pastors' conference. The religious department in the police had found out about the gathering and burst into the meeting room with guns at the ready. They arrested the leaders, took them away and gave them a beating. He too was arrested, but as a foreigner was detained in a cell while they did some investigating as to what exactly he was doing there. He somehow managed to get a message to a friend, and that friend happened to have some connections high up in government there. A message was soon relayed to the local police chief and he ended up being treated politely, though told he now had just 24 hours to get out of the country.

   You may have seen some opposition in your life. Who is it that God has provided for you to protect and support you? Let us thank God for those friends and acquaintances who show us love, even protection when we are under pressure from someone opposed to us. My friend in the police cell was shown love by someone in high office. Who knows, maybe one day you'll find yourself in a position to help someone practically who is suffering opposition.

3. We need to apply some common sense as well. David eluded Saul's murderous attempts. Twice. He didn't just sit there. Jesus also took practical measures to avoid arrest until his time had come (John 7:1-19).

4. We've already seen the importance of allowing ourselves to be drawn to consider the suffering of our Lord when opposed by sinners. We would have been among them had we been there, or like his disciples would have disappeared, or denied him. This should strengthen us. He has forgiven us our sins – sins that he died for, our soul that he died for. Will he not also along with him, freely give us all things? That includes strength to face opposition

and not give in. And even if we do, like Peter did in denying the Lord three times, we can be assured that the Lord is willing to restore us (John 18:1-27 & 21:15-19).

5. As he was with David, let us give thanks to God for his Spirit, that *He is with us*. God is with us his children in the general sense – that is his promise.

6. A related point. Are you *being filled* with the Spirit? Peter and Paul, the two most prominent leaders and speakers in the early church were often filled with the Spirit. For example Acts 4:8 and 13:9. Why does it say they were filled, and filled more than once? Because it is vital for ministry, and because it is possible *not* to be filled, to be empty. It's why the literal sense in the original language of Ephesians 5:18 is the command to *go on letting ourselves be filled.* It's something that is done to us, something done to a group of people. Ephesians was written to an entire church, and let's not forget that the nucleus of that church – 12 men – were all filled with the Spirit *at the same time* (Acts 19:1-7). It's the exact same sense in Ephesians 6:10…'go on being made strong', namely, in his mighty power. It's something we need to keep let happening to us, to keep letting ourselves be filled by the Spirit, to keep holding out our cup as it were, for God to fill it. We cannot fill ourselves.

7. In Saul there's a warning for us too about losing the anointing and actually ending up being opposed to God's purposes. This could be due to fear or jealousy, or even over something we've come to deeply value, even our own traditions, or something else that spills over and seeks to damage those we should love. Yes, Jesus will never leave us or forsake us, but that does not mean we can't end up in sin, thus losing God's power in whatever sphere of service he has called us to. Samson's life also stands as a clear warning in that regard. And he did not realise that the anointing had left him until it was too late (Judges 16:20). He was allowed to persist in sin for a time, but it all finally caught up with him.

A foothold

One young man became so enraged over an incident in which he felt he'd been mistreated by another believer that God allowed him to become oppressed by an evil spirit. It went far beyond being bitter: he let his anger spill over for several days and the enemy was allowed to get a foothold (Ephesians 4:26-27). He went on to share how he later repented and immediately felt a massive sense of release. As he prayed, he could clearly sense the oppressive force that had been bearing down on him literally coming off his shoulders and leaving him. He had not been taught that God could allow such spiritual oppression, but his experience taught him that an evil spirit had indeed been allowed to afflict him for a season, and was removed when he repented. It was not simply guilt he was released from. He learned an important lesson about the nature and offence of sin, and how God can sometimes deal with people, including his children, by allowing spiritual oppression by the enemy. (Was it not the same for the nation of Israel if they repeatedly rebelled? One of the ways God disciplined Israel was to allow surrounding nations to invade parts of her territory, and at the end the entire country, taking most of the occupants into exile. Other methods included famine.)

The young man did not consider himself demonised (not 'demon-possessed' as some translations have it, for the Scripture says, 'The earth is the Lord's and everything in it' – Psalm 24:1). He was more harassed or afflicted by an evil spirit, with God's permission. The account of Abimelech and the citizens of Shechem in Judges chapter 9 is instructive in this matter. God allowed a bad spirit to come between the two parties in order to bring judgment upon them (verses 23-24).

And to conclude, in all this we walk with our Lord the Victor who fought against sin during terrible opposition and yet won via the cross, and now sits at the right hand of the Father as the Priest and King interceding for us, including when we fall. Hallelujah! Isn't that continuing good news.

QUESTIONS FOR REFLECTION OR DISCUSSION

1. Are you at risk of jealousy or fear of someone whom God is clearly blessing more than you?

2. If you've not done so already, take a moment to look up to Christ who endured such opposition from sinful people in going to and staying on the cross. This is important for us so that we don't grow weary and lose heart (Hebrews 12:3).

3. Recount a time when you tried to do the will of God, only to be opposed by someone?

4. Recall how God strengthened you either directly by his Spirit or by providing someone to bless or protect you. It could be something as simple as an encouraging email or message by some other medium.

5. Is there someone suffering for doing the will of God that you could strengthen somehow? We should pray for those suffering for their faith, and if we can offer practical support as well to do so.

6. Are you seeking to be filled with the Spirit? We saw from our very brief look at Acts that it is not a one-off. And it is something that happens to us.[26]

---

26. For more on this I recommend Martyn Lloyd-Jones' book *Joy Unspeakable* where he argues for an actual experience of the Spirit subsequent to conversion. He was a noted expositor of the Bible, and coming from a more traditional background became convinced that the baptism is the Spirit is, in the word of one of the chapters in the book, 'Something that happens to us'.

PART TWO: FUGITIVE

FROM THIS POINT on, David has fled from Saul. He now knows for sure that it's simply too dangerous to even attempt to stay around. He is on the run – a fugitive. But God is with him, and part of that long, testing period involved being assaulted by various emotions as he was hunted down, or as we shall see firstly, brushed off as a rebel. It is during this period that David penned his richest words. Out of the fire, gold. Treating every single episode would make for far too a long a book, so we will look at a few choice episodes, including a psalm which looks at the topic of depression.

CHAPTER

6

RESTRAINING ANGER

Anger is a very intense but tiny emotion, you know. It doesn't last. It doesn't produce anything. It's not creative ... at least not for me.[27]

Toni Morrison, Author

Human anger does not produce the righteousness that God desires.

James 1:20

DAVID HAD EVERY right to be angry about the way he had been treated by Saul. More than once God gave him a clear opportunity to take revenge and kill him. David would not harm the Lord's anointed, King Saul. But how would he respond when someone far less important offended him?

As we pick up the story, we are told that the elderly prophet Samuel had died. Samuel had been highly regarded by the people, but David had known him personally. It would have been a big blow for him. The person who best understood his destiny, the man who had picked him out and anointed him as the future king, was dead. A spiritual giant in

27. https://www.theparisreview.org/interviews/1888/the-art-of-fiction-no-134-toni-morrison Accessed 2nd June, 2021.

the land and personal mentor to David…gone. David moved further away into the desert to put greater distance between himself and Saul.

The Scripture doesn't record if David got to the funeral of Samuel, but it is unlikely given the circumstances. He would have needed to be in disguise since Saul was out to kill him. So David likely didn't get to say a final goodbye in the normal manner to an important mentor. Perhaps you can relate.

The first reading in this chapter is from 1st Samuel chapter 25 verses 1-12.

> *Now Samuel (the prophet) died, and all Israel assembled and mourned for him; and they buried him at his home in Ramah. Then David moved down into the Desert of Paran.*
>
> *A certain man in Maon, who had property there at Carmel, was very wealthy. He had a thousand goats and three thousand sheep, which he was shearing in Carmel. His name was Nabal and his wife's name was Abigail. She was an intelligent and beautiful woman, but her husband was surly and mean in his dealings—he was a Calebite.*
>
> *While David was in the wilderness, he heard that Nabal was shearing sheep. So he sent ten young men and said to them, "Go up to Nabal at Carmel and greet him in my name. Say to him: 'Long life to you! Good health to you and your household! And good health to all that is yours!*
>
> *"'Now I hear that it is sheep-shearing time. When your shepherds were with us, we did not mistreat them, and the whole time they were at Carmel nothing of theirs was missing. Ask your own servants and they will tell you. Therefore be favourable toward my men, since we come at a festive time. Please give your servants and your son David whatever you can find for them.'"*
>
> *When David's men arrived, they gave Nabal this message in David's name. Then they waited.*

Nabal answered David's servants, "Who is this David? Who is this son of Jesse? Many servants are breaking away from their masters (Saul) these days. Why should I take my bread and water, and the meat I have slaughtered for my shearers, and give it to men coming from who knows where?"

David's men turned around and went back. When they arrived, they reported every word. David said to his men, "Each of you strap on your sword!" So they did, and David strapped his on as well. About four hundred men went up with David, while two hundred stayed with the supplies.

1 Samuel 25:1-12 (my inserts in brackets for clarification)

Most of us know of people who have 'lost it' when they are angry. Younger workers can be crushed under the weight of harsh and unjust criticism by a senior manager. An angry boss may shout at staff but pay for it years later by a gradual loss of reputation. Maybe you were the one who lost their temper. Perhaps it was a relationship outside of the workplace, and things have not been the same since.

Anger is a powerful emotion: unchecked, unrighteous anger can do considerable damage. Whether damaging a relationship or losing a job, such outbursts come with consequences. Diplomacy often saves the day; unrestrained anger can ruin it.

DAVID'S RESPONSE

Losing your cool

Why did David fly off the handle? Having tackled lions and bears, Goliath and many Philistines he certainly knew about violence, but this was different. Grumpy Nabal was no threat to him. Was it because David had been denied something before, and now felt entitled? Saul had promised David his daughter Michal in marriage, but afterwards handed her off to someone else once David fled the royal court. Maybe David felt like he was owed something in life, deserved a break. It's not like he deserved to be hunted down. Was he just fed up being on the run? Maybe he and his men were simply hungry; maybe all of these. Thankfully we don't need to guess, and providentially, David is literally stopped in his tracks by the beautiful and quick-thinking Abigail, Nabal's long-suffering wife.

> One of the servants told Abigail, Nabal's wife, "David sent messengers from the wilderness to give our master his greetings, but he hurled insults at them. Yet these men were very good to us. They did not mistreat us, and the whole time we were out in the fields near them nothing was missing. Night and day they were a wall around us the whole time we were herding our sheep near them. Now think it over and see what you can do, because disaster is hanging over our master and his whole household. He is such a wicked man that no one can talk to him."
>
> Abigail acted quickly. She took two hundred loaves of bread, two skins of wine, five dressed sheep, five seahs (around 60 lbs or 27kg) of roasted grain, a hundred cakes of raisins and two hundred cakes of pressed figs, and loaded them on donkeys. Then she told her servants, "Go on ahead; I'll follow you." But she did not tell her husband Nabal.
>
> As she came riding her donkey into a mountain ravine, there were David and his men descending toward her, and she met them. David had just said, "It's been useless—all my watching over this fellow's property in the wilderness so that nothing of his was missing. He has paid me back evil for good. May God deal with David, be it ever so severely, if by morning I leave alive one male of all who belong to him!"

1 Samuel 25:13-22 (my insert in brackets)

Having acted honourably in protecting Nabal's sheep and being like a wall around his men, Nabal's words were like a match lighting a fuse. David was incensed by Nabal's reply the messengers brought back.

'It's been useless!' he exclaimed.

Maybe you've heard a similar statement by someone who is angry about something and is about to give up completely. Or lash out. From the rest of his words we see that David felt he had at least earned some leftovers from the exceptionally wealthy Nabal at such an abundant time during summer when the sheep-shearers were being fed and thanked for their hard work. There was ample food about. Culturally, it would be expected to provide for those protecting you.

> '*It's been useless—all my watching over this fellow's property in the wilderness so that nothing of his was missing.*'

Nabal had thousands of cattle. Just a few of them roasted and carved up would have fed all of David's men. Nabal wasn't even being asked to arrange the cooking! David's 'night-shift' team had prevented Nabal from losing stock to predators, both human and animal. The behaviour of David and his men had been exemplary.

David told his men to strap on their swords – so they did. So did he. Three times in the original the word 'sword' appears. David meant business, and it was personal. A rich landowner with a few men would be no match for David and his hundreds of men.

The fool

Nabal was a stupid man. He knew David's reputation as a brave fighter, having famously defeated Goliath some years before, having had his name put to song, and having had successful command of a large unit of men for a season before going on the run. His reply to David's messengers shows us that he knew David had left Saul. In it he questions David's identity, his background, and he calls him a rebel – a runaway servant. Humanly speaking, that's how you might perceive David. But even on *that* level why would you want to get on the wrong side of someone who had done *you* no wrong, especially a highly capable, young military leader with hundreds of men, essentially operating as a guerrilla in the countryside?[28] More importantly, spiritually speaking Nabal did not recognise that God's hand was on

---

28. I appreciate that the term guerrilla does not belong to that era (an anachronism) but I've left it in for effect for the reader. A battalion in the US Army can be up to 1,000 soldiers; in the British Army it is up to 650. It was a sizable group of men used to fighting and surviving.

David. His foolishness extended to failing to recognise the anointed one. And imagine the stories he could have told his grandchildren and the royal connection he could have made had he simply provided for David and his men?

Whichever side you took, if someone with *that* reputation and *that* many fighting men in your backyard had the good grace to not only have his men refrain from touching your flocks but instead help protect them, then at harvest time you might want to show your appreciation by offering them even some leftovers; after all, there was plenty going about. As noted already, given the hospitality culture of the time it would have not only been reasonable to offer David some food, but expected. A man in his position might even have made a friend for life, aiding someone in dire straits. But not foolish Nabal. He showed contempt and was true to his name: someone mean and surly in dealing with others.

Isn't it amazing the dumb things people can do? Nabal wasn't so much 'shooting himself in the foot' by being rude to David as inviting him to slice open his stomach with his sword. He added not only insult to injury, but growing hunger.

His wife, Abigail, provides a stunning contrast in more ways than one. Her actions and plea are deeply instructive for all developing leaders who need a timely and arresting reminder that their destiny is not in their own hands, despite what some may claim. Yes, our actions effect our future, but we cannot create our own destiny. It is God who works in us to will and act according to his good purpose (Philippians 2:13); it is *he* who has prepared good works in advance for us to do. We are *his* workmanship (Ephesians 2:10).

Nabal's life would seem to have been in David's hands, but David's life was in someone else's. What would he do? Would he be rash like Saul? Would he *restrain* himself like he done with Saul, refusing to kill the Lord's anointed, the present king? Saul, King of Israel was one thing, but a rich and unprotected farmer?

The story continues…

When Abigail saw David, she quickly got off her donkey and bowed down before David with her face to the ground. She fell at his feet and said: "Pardon your servant, my lord, and let me speak to you; hear what your servant has to say. Please pay no attention, my lord, to that wicked man Nabal. He is just like his name—his name means Fool, and folly goes with him. And as for me, your servant, I did not see the men my lord sent. And now, my lord, as surely as the LORD your God lives and as you live, since the LORD has kept you from bloodshed and from avenging yourself with your own hands, may your enemies and all who are intent on harming my lord be like Nabal. And let this gift, which your servant has brought to my lord, be given to the men who follow you.

"Please forgive your servant's presumption. The LORD your God will certainly make a lasting dynasty for my lord, because you fight the LORD's battles, and no wrongdoing will be found in you as long as you live. Even though someone is pursuing you to take your life, the life of my lord will be bound securely in the bundle of the living by the LORD your God, but the lives of your enemies he will hurl away as from the pocket of a sling. When the LORD has fulfilled for my lord every good thing he promised concerning him and has appointed him ruler over Israel, my lord will not have on his conscience the staggering burden of needless bloodshed or of having avenged himself. And when the LORD your God has brought my lord success, remember your servant."

1 Samuel 25:23-31

ABIGAIL, CHRIST, AND THE PRACTICAL RELEVANCE

This time I've threaded in some pertinent and practical questions as we consider the narrative and how it reflects some aspect of the good news of Jesus, the gospel.

The contrast

Nabal was foolish, Abigail wise. Stupid vs. Sensible. Mean vs. Generous. She was also attractive on the outside. Quickly realising that someone like David, enraged *and* with a small army at his disposal might actually be someone to make glad and not mad she rushed to placate him. Saving her husband's neck and those of all Nabal's men she did a quick mass catering job – plenty of food available during all those festivities as we've seen. It's why the food is carefully listed for us: it underlines what Nabal *failed* to provide. It was not some protection racket David was operating.

On meeting David, Abigail prostrated herself and made a lengthy plea. Her appeal was like a cool hand on a hot head. Her words are recorded at length to instruct us as regards not only checking our own anger, but soothing the anger of others about to discharge it like a double-barrelled shotgun. Here we consider her words and ask some pertinent questions about restraining anger, and Abigail's intervention on behalf of her husband and how it can help us consider our wonderful Saviour. In the next (shorter) chapter we'll consider in some detail how we can process our own anger using other means God graciously provides, and how that can help us lean on the Lord.

1. She sent food for David and his men ahead of her. They say that the way to a man's heart is through his stomach. Well it seems too that the way to get into David's *head* was also through his stomach. Hunger can be a strong driving force. 'Hangry' I heard one parent term it recently when referring to their hungry and angry toddler. Abigail was also acutely aware of the expectation that some food *should* have been provided by Nabal in the first place. This was the key cultural matter of offense she was seeking to address. Urgently. Her actions made up for her husband's shortcomings and showed appreciation for and hospitality toward David and his men.

    Which immediate need or culturally sensitive action might you take to mollify someone you've really offended? The proverb says, "An angry man is silenced by giving him a gift"(Proverbs 21:14). Those working in cross-cultural situations will be more aware of this, but there's a practical point here for leaders and pastors, young and old, ministering in their own cultural contexts: inviting someone for food is often a wise way to help placate an offended brother or sister or colleague (or perhaps even some customer / client). Listening to their complaint shows that you care. And doing it over food makes it slower. It's hard to lose the rag over chocolate dessert or some other delicacy. It's not about being manipulative but providing a context in which the offended person can process their anger or frustration.

I once sat for three hours over lunch in a restaurant with an offended youth leader. A pleasant environment was no guarantee of winning her over, but it certainly helped to do so. The length to which I was prepared to hear her out and discuss her burning issue and address her own attitude at the same time was incredibly important. Thankfully, I'd got some great advice from a more experienced pastor beforehand: Hear them out, ask questions, don't rush. And it's not the first time I've had to do this.

Food and fellowship go together like bread and butter (or choose your own cultural pairing). So, add the food and pray the fellowship will develop as you process the issue together. It is like a cool hand on a hot head.

2. Abigail surrendered before David: she fell at his feet and offered an apology. "Let the blame be on me alone," some translations render it. Abigail foreshadowed Christ by interceding on behalf of another (Nabal) who had caused huge offense. Humanity is guilty and under God's judgment for sin. The New Testament makes it clear that when Jesus died on the cross, he took on himself God's *righteous* anger against sinners (as opposed to David's *rash* anger) and that this holy anger was successfully appeased (Romans 3:25-26).

"Let the blame be on me alone."

What's even more incredible is that the triune God planned all along to present Christ as a sacrifice to turn away the wrath of God against mankind in order to satisfy his justice, and justify sinners.[29] This is the heart of the cross of Christ.

Under the influence of the Spirit, Isaiah also predicted the plan some seven hundred years before it actually took place.

Yet it was the Lord's will to crush him and cause him to suffer,
and though the Lord makes his life an offering for sin,
he will see his offspring and prolong his days,
and the will of the Lord will prosper in his hand.
After he has suffered,
he will see the light of life and be satisfied;
by his knowledge my righteous servant will justify many,
and he will bear their iniquities.
Therefore I will give him a portion among the great,
and he will divide the spoils with the strong,
because he poured out his life unto death,
and was numbered with the transgressors.
For he bore the sin of many,
and made intercession for the transgressors.

Isaiah 53:10-12

3. Abigail pointed to the obvious: Providence.

"Since the Lord has kept you from bloodshed and from avenging yourself with your own hands."

Her arrival was no mere coincidence. Ravines are narrow – they couldn't miss each other. *God* had sent her in time to stop an irate man in his tracks. When you're in a rage you can't see sense. God graciously provided someone to block his path, to prevent him from going *way* overboard. You or someone you know may have a similar story.

4. Abigail pointed out that David had no history of taking matters into his own hands, i.e. 'This isn't you, David. This isn't a fight

---

29. What's known as 'propitiation' or a 'sacrifice of atonement'. Romans 3:25

you should be getting into. Wrong battle!' Had he not recently refrained from killing Saul when he had an easy opportunity to do so? (yes). And as he had restrained himself before and turned to the Lord, could not David again let *God* deal with this offense? (yes). Stating that *the Lord* would deal with David's enemies and hurl them away 'as from the pocket of a sling' was not only incisive, but softening. The image referred of course to David's victory over the giant Goliath some years earlier – an intelligent woman indeed. David generally fought the right battles: the Lord's. David's life was securely in the hands of God who would clear the way for him to be crowned king one day.

Do you need to urge someone to avoid sinful conflict – for there *is* such a thing as *healthy* conflict – by pointing out their good track record so far and how the Lord has their back?

5. Abigail appealed to him to trust God and keep his future leadership as stain-free as possible. Major mistakes in your first half can carry over into your second. Some people have had to leave town over abuse or misuse of people or staff, and thus put the good news in a bad light.

Things can come back to haunt us, or a leader who succeeds us. I watched from a distance one situation where decisions made by a local church leadership unravelled and imploded in on the congregation *seven years after* the main leaders left. Those new to the church will have had little idea that the root of the issue went right back to decisions by previous leaders. David later experienced this dynamic in a far more deadly form when God poured judgment out on the country years after a predecessor's error; in his zeal, Saul had tried to destroy a community of people who had been promised protection.[30]

Consider any case of the abuse of power, whether sexual, spiritual, emotional or physical, etc, brought to court recently. As well as impaired lives, it destroys the reputation of the guilty

---

30. 2 Samuel 21 records how God allowed a three-year famine across the nation because of Saul, David's predecessor's sin of killing the Gibeonites with whom the Israelites had a long-standing peace treaty (Joshua 9).

party who up until that point was respected. Their decades-long leadership or standing may quickly unravel. So, is there someone you know in a position of trust considering abusing or currently abusing their power? Like Abigail, do not delay! Unlike David, maybe they've already been abusive. If so, what can you do to step in, or in the case of clear abuse inform the relevant authorities?

6. Last, Abigail believed in David. *'When the Lord your God has brought you success.'* Not *if.* Had Samuel been there he might have well said similar words, or by his mere presence been a restraining factor in David's leadership. What a woman! Our greatest enemy is often ourselves. How fortunate for David to encounter Abigail. How gracious of God to send her. An unexpected rendezvous in a ravine.

Whether you're a promising young leader or a mentor to one, after perhaps some practical steps to placate someone else (i.e. food!) are you in a position to reason with an angry or really upset person and state your conviction about their calling, whatever that may be? If you win them over, they'll thank you for it in the long run. You will have saved them from the staggering burden of a massive first- or indeed second-half mistake. As importantly, you will have been the instrument through which God highlights his saving grace in Christ. It is *God* who avenges and protects us. And it is God who fulfilled every good thing concerning his Son the Lord Jesus and appointed him as King of the whole earth by his resurrection and ascension. The Lord is king!

QUESTIONS FOR REFLECTION OR DISCUSSION

1. You've read or listened to David's story. Recount a story you or someone else know about when someone else became enraged but was saved from going overboard by someone else. It could be in a book, a film, or in real life.

2. Recount a time you have been an 'Abigail' to someone else who was really angry.

3. Is there someone now that you need to be an Abigail to?

4. Let's stop and give thanks for God's wonderful intercessor, Jesus, who stood on our behalf to turn away the righteous wrath of God for our sins.

CHAPTER

7

PROCESSING ANGER

Even the finest sword plunged into salt water will eventually rust.

The Art of War – Sun Tzu

Get rid of….all rage and anger.

Ephesians 5:31

David said to Abigail, "Praise be to the LORD, the God of Israel, who has sent you today to meet me. May you be blessed for your good judgment and for keeping me from bloodshed this day and from avenging myself with my own hands. Otherwise, as surely as the LORD, the God of Israel, lives, who has kept me from harming you, if you had not come quickly to meet me, not one male belonging to Nabal would have been left alive by daybreak."

Then David accepted from her hand what she had brought him and said, "Go home in peace. I have heard your words and granted your request."

When Abigail went to Nabal, he was in the house holding a banquet like that of a king. He was in high spirits and very drunk. So she told him nothing at all until daybreak. Then in the morning, when Nabal was sober, his wife told him all these things, and his heart failed him and he became like a stone. About ten days later, the LORD struck Nabal and he died.

When David heard that Nabal was dead, he said, "Praise be to the LORD, who has upheld my cause against Nabal for treating me with contempt. He has kept his servant from doing wrong and has brought Nabal's wrongdoing down on his own head."

Then David sent word to Abigail, asking her to become his wife. His servants went to Carmel and said to Abigail, "David has sent us to you to take you to become his wife."

She bowed down with her face to the ground and said, "I am your servant and am ready to serve you and wash the feet of my lord's servants." Abigail quickly got on a donkey, and attended by her five female servants, went with David's messengers and became his wife. David had also married Ahinoam of Jezreel, and they both were his wives. But Saul had given his daughter Michal, David's wife, to Paltiel son of Laish, who was from Gallim.

1 Samuel 25:32-44

DAVID'S CONTEXT AND OURS

FILLED WITH ANGER and with a clinched fist, you've sworn to let a customer you've bent over backwards to help have it: you're going to break his nose. He has greatly offended you as well as short-changing your company of money. It's late in the day, you're hungry, and so is your team. As you charge out of out the office door shouting to your colleagues about why you even bother, a delivery arrives – a massive order of the highest quality pizzas, enough for everyone still in the building. A beautiful and modest woman you've never met follows immediately after the food, and pleads with you to show mercy and deal kindly with her husband – the man who has offended you. Her actions speak to you far more than her beauty. The combination stops you in your tracks and forces you to reconsider. You recognise the hand of God in the situation…and stop. Your anger subsides and your leadership, not to mention your conscience, is saved from needless harm and guilt. But you nearly blew it, and you realise again your shortcomings. You may have worked hard, have considerable responsibility, been called to a high task, been anointed by God, but you are deeply flawed.

Such was David's experience. His response has something to teach us about how we process our anger, and that we need to recognise God's grace in providing a way out for us to deal with it. As in David's case, that kindness might come in some dramatic form, but more often it may be simpler, like 'a word in our ear' from a brother or sister, or even a random comment from someone who has no idea about what we are feeling or what we've been doing. Despite his many excellent qualities, the episode also further underlines the need for another king of an altogether different order.

Leadership and emotional capacity

The building of your emotional and spiritual capacity – to use a more contemporary term – is crucial to fostering a church or organisation's capacity. Generally speaking, as the leaders go, so do the people. This is a clear secondary message of David versus Goliath. Saul was afraid; so was everyone else. A leader who acts impetuously out of fear or anger will cause unnecessary conflict and soon lead people into the wrong battles: needless aggravation.

David's emotional and leadership capacity was being stretched, and it took intervention to prevent him from making a major blunder. He responded by listening to sound advice when about to act rashly. He failed the first part of the test (Nabal's foolish and insensitive reply to the men David had sent to ask for food), but he passed the second (recognising the divine interruption that helped prevent him from carrying out his bloody intent).

Anger is something that as a leader in your first half, and disciple of the Lord Jesus, you will need to develop an inner capacity to deal with. Those serving in some form of leadership role can lose their anointing by failing to work through it or lashing out when they come under pressure. The issue here is dealing with the root issue inside of us. For

David, the temptation was to break out in anger and take revenge; for Saul, as we learned previously, it was reacting out of fear, and he often succumbed and rebelled against God.

Anger has to go somewhere, be expressed somehow, whether you are someone who tends to express your anger or not. Unless it's over some small matter it doesn't just go away. Whatever the type of anger we feel, we need to process it in a healthy way. In this chapter we briefly consider more routine, but no less important ways God provides grace for us to recognise and work through our anger.

A soft pillow

A good type of anger is righteous indignation, when you are justifiably angry; for example, someone has mistreated someone you know, or you. You may not have sinned in the process of being angry. We often see this in those pursuing a just cause to defend the weak or innocent. It may well mean you will have to still process some hurt they caused you, or someone you love – the anger you feel is a result of that hurt. But it may be because your fellow leaders or team have badly underperformed – they *can* do a lot better. You may even be angry at yourself.

It's why we can sometimes wake up in the morning with a certain person's name or image in our head. That's actually a good thing, and it can happen if we have sinned in our anger, or if we have *not* sinned. It's God's way of telling us there's an issue to deal with, for us to bring it to God.

One of David's journal entries says this:

> *Be angry, and do not sin; ponder in your own hearts on your beds, and be silent. Offer right sacrifices, and put your trust in the Lord.*
> **Psalm 4:4-5**

It literally says to 'speak', i.e. ponder within your own heart, but be silent (not speak it out to others). This encourages us to process it. It's when we stop – which we have to in bed – that we often find ourselves alone with our own thoughts. It's sometimes why God will allow us to be isolated; it provides time to think. The deeper issues often come to the surface of our minds. This too is part of God's gracious provision. If a clear conscience is like a soft pillow, then a troubled one is like a brick. We just can't get back to sleep. As uncomfortable or annoying as it may be because we are tired, our unsettledness is a sign something is amiss. We can take it to God in prayer.

Grenades and casseroles

Another type of human but sinful anger is *rage* (Ephesians 4:31). This is what David experienced when he heard Nabal's reply. You can only see red. It's like taking the pin out of a grenade. It's the same word in Ephesians that is used to describe the *rage* the people in the synagogue felt when Jesus read out that prophesy from Isaiah; it drove them to drag him to the top of a local cliff to throw him off it. We've seen how God graciously provided for David; in the case of our Lord it simply says that he walked back right through the middle of them (Luke 4:30).

Another related type of anger is what you could call *casserole* or *stew* type anger simmering under the surface. It may be on the back burner out of sight, but it's there. It often stems from unforgiveness and can go on for years, even decades, and dominate a person's life.

Dealing with your own anger

Depending on your personality and the situation or person whose actions you are angry about, dealing with it in real-time, or soon after, is best. Abigail intervened and calmed David down with lots of great food and carefully chosen words. She helped David deal with it promptly.

Yet dealing with it right away may be hard, and in some cases impossible. For example, can a child abused by a family member deal with it *as* they are growing up? What about those suffering the trauma of the violence of war? What about those struggling after an intense and difficult period in the workplace? Can they take time out and deal with any anger *during* the heat of battle? Perhaps, perhaps not. Sometimes they can't because there is simply too much happening round about them, or they don't know what to do, or they're too young to process it at the time. They have to wait and deal with it later on, perhaps much later. Some may not be fully aware of just how deeply angry they are, because they are not yet fully aware of how deeply hurt they are.

Find a person, place or practice

Anger can manifest itself in various ways. If you are angry, you could ask yourself *who specifically* could be a cool hand on your hot or troubled head. Maybe someone good at counselling. Like Abigail they are going to have to be someone who offers you a way to deal with your anger, feeds your soul, perhaps also your body, and encourages you about the future pointing you heavenward.

For many men, a godly wife can offer this, but perhaps you may need other help from someone more used to dealing with it, someone with more experience in counselling. You may find you need to write things out in order to fully process everything. If you are depressed you may need medication for a time. Maybe all of these things. Whatever, I'd encourage you to learn to process your anger. You will have a healthier first, and certainly healthier second half if you do, since you will have learned some valuable lessons. Let God and others he sends your way – maybe right under your nose – help you deal with your anger.

SOMEONE GREATER

We saw in the previous chapter David's shortcomings. We also saw in Abigail God's provision, and in that way, she points us to a greater and more perfect intercessor who intercedes for us in our flawed state, the foolishness of sinning against the Almighty.

Jesus too was tested. His perfect pass-rate makes him the perfect and holy leader to spiritually draw on through faith. He knows what it is to suffer when being tempted. Because of his suffering he is able to help those being tempted, and that includes those times when we may be tempted to lash out in anger because we are hurt or offended, or when some issue is simmering away below the surface (Hebrews 2:18). As Hebrews makes clear, he is the Great High Priest. Moreover, he is the king in the order of Melchizedek, one who brings peace (Hebrews 7:2). We later read of David donning a ephod (priestly clothing) when he brings the ark into Jerusalem (2 Samuel 6). It's a wonderful picture of the role of king *and* priest being merged together, and one which we see perfected and fulfilled in Jesus.

When Jesus was arrested and put on trial, Peter, one his leading disciples, pulled out his sword and sliced off one of the arresting party's ears.

Jesus responded:

> *"Put away your sword....those using swords will get killed. Don't you realize that I could ask my Father for thousands of angels to protect us, and he would send them instantly?"*
>
> **Matthew 26:52-53 (The Living Bible)**

Abigail was not able to summon angels, but by her actions she conveyed a similar message to David: put away your sword. But we see Jesus' restraint supremely before and during the affliction of the cross. Provoked and mocked when in great anguish he could have called on the Father to send angels to free him and wipe out those who so cruelly harmed him. Along with them, our sin created the horrible need for his sacrificial death.

Isaiah the prophet predicted many years before his death:

> *He was oppressed and he was afflicted, yet he never said a word. He was brought as a lamb to the slaughter; and as a sheep before her shearers is dumb, so he stood silent before the ones condemning him.*
>
> **Isaiah 53:7**

As we considered in the previous chapter, here is also how we see the anger of God poured out on his dear Son for us. How marvellous and astounding. Propitiation: turning away wrath by means of a sacrifice (Romans 3:25). Let us give thanks for our wonderful Saviour who took on Himself the wrath of God as a sin-offering for us, and who now serves as King and everlasting Great High Priest who always intercedes for us (Hebrews 7:25).

QUESTIONS FOR REFLECTION OR DISCUSSION

1. We all react differently. Which type of anger (an explosive grenade or a simmering casserole) do you think you are most like when you are genuinely hurt by someone or something?

2. When you have processed your anger well, how have you done that?

3. If you realise that you need help now, *who* could be like an Abigail to you?

4. How specifically could you bring some of David's story and journal entries to bear on how you process your anger in your relationship with God and help you 'put away your sword'?

5. Again, let's consider Jesus who suffered such great hurt and anger when tempted and has now gone through the heavens, a Great High Priest whom we can now turn to when we are being tempted (Hebrews 2:10).

CHAPTER

8

ISOLATION AND DEPRESSION

How long, LORD? Will you forget me forever?
  How long will you hide your face from me?
How long must I wrestle with my thoughts
  and day after day have sorrow in my heart?
  How long will my enemy triumph over me?

Look on me and answer (me), LORD my God.
  Give light to my eyes, or I will sleep in death,
and my enemy will say, "I have overcome him," and my foes will
rejoice when I fall.

But I trust in your unfailing love;
  my heart rejoices in your salvation.
I will sing the LORD's praise,
  for he has been good to me.

Psalm 13 (my insert)

DEPRESSION AND 'SOUL EXERCISE'

HAVE YOU EVER been forgotten or felt forgotten about? Not nice, is it? Your one constant friend may be your own thoughts, some of which may be downright ugly. And yet an important stage in the development of anyone who ends up being a major influence on others is that in his sovereignty God may allow them to be isolated at times. If that's your situation then you're in good company. It could be because of illness, some form of persecution, misunderstanding or rejection. For example, the first black president of South Africa, Nelson Mandela, spent many years in prison before he became president. Watchman Nee, a major figure in the history of the Church in China, spent 20 years in prison for leading churches in a Communist state. At one point the apostle Paul was imprisoned and then completely abandoned by many he expected would have stood by him. His writing of that experience near the end of his life facing trial has comforted many in similar circumstances down the centuries (the end of his second letter to Timothy).

Isolation can also lead to depression, something that can cripple a person's mental health. This is where the psalms in the Bible can be so helpful. Reading them is like pondering written records of not physical but 'soul-exercises' which we can then put into practice. Indeed, some ancient Christian leaders called the psalms the 'gymnasium for the soul'. Just as the human body can be trained by intense physical exercise, so too is the soul when stretched and put under pressure: pain, joy, anger, frustration, love, hatred, envy, gloom, and faith can all emerge. In the psalms we see people of faith stretched and pulled and put through their paces, wrestling with God through it all. Moreover, as with the rest of Scripture, they're designed to lead us to Christ. Indeed, some commentators see all the psalms ultimately as the prayers of Christ, not just the ones (or the verses) that directly speak of or predict some aspect of the Saviour's life, suffering, death or resurrection.

DAVID'S EXPERIENCE

As a young lad, David was anointed by the prophet Samuel as the future king. He probably didn't imagine it would take around 20 years for that prophecy to be fulfilled when he was crowned king at the age of 37. Not weeks, months, years, but decades. That's tough leadership training for you.

But whatever the circumstances for each person, it's not an

overnight process. God is in no hurry to shape those whom he uses, especially those in more public roles. And that of course is not limited to those to whom God has given the gift of leadership whose role may be more front facing (Romans 12:8). Indeed, the route may be far longer than desired, and in the process of such training younger leaders can feel incredibly isolated at times. This can be true of those who value teamwork and prefer not to work in isolation. They too can find themselves in very lonely places in spirit, even with good people around them or alongside them.

Psalm 13 is one psalm, a song in this instance, among a few in the psalms that are particularly helpful in assisting those, including those called and gifted to lead, who find themselves in a dark or isolated place. The words can comfort those who feel forgotten and help them recognise what to do and where to ultimately put their trust. We can apply David's words to situations in which we feel we can't see when or how our struggle will end, or where God fits in it all. David wrote about the agony of waiting and waiting...and waiting. It communicates his great depths of despair and sense of 'divine' abandonment.

How Long x 4

In this song David fires off a barrage of questions towards heaven. It's the stuff of taut anguish. Four times he asks painfully, 'How long?' He can see no end to his inner turmoil, no light at the end of the tunnel. He feels forgotten. It's like God does not want to see him anymore; the Almighty has turned his back on him. Threatened by black clouds surrounding him, his mind meanders among dark shadows. He's utterly miserable, and it goes on, day after day after day after day.

Do you know what that feels like? In such times your sleeping patterns can get disturbed, perhaps your eating patterns too. Sexual attraction or interest can wane. Wrestling, fighting with your thoughts every day. It's like being in the ring with a strong opponent every day, except he's inside your head. British wartime leader Winston Churchill called his occasional periods of depression the 'black dog'.[31] What for

31. https://winstonchurchill.org/publications/finest-hour/finest-hour-155/the-myth-of-the-black-dog/

some may be occasional and mild, may for others be more deep and enduring.

CHRIST IN THE PSALMS

As with the rest of Scripture, God placed the psalms – the prayers and songs of God's people – in the Bible in order to point people to Christ. The fact that more than half the psalms are attributed to David, a king, means they are a rich and necessary feature of this book. His flawed ministry as a king only underlined the need for someone much greater, and God later promised David that through one of his descendants he would build a house for his own name, that this Son of David would have an everlasting kingdom. In this way, God would build a house, a dynasty for David, and establish the throne of his kingdom forever. That the kingdom was torn in two within two generations after David pointed to one more enduring, a different son altogether, but one descended from David, with his DNA in his body. We explore this in chapter 13 when we look at 2 Samuel 7.

As the royal Son of David, Jesus knows what it is to be tempted and tested, battle it out *and win*. The psalms can help us when wrestling with such thoughts, and how we can pray with Jesus as the One who has faced all possible types of temptations and trials.

The book of Hebrews makes it abundantly clear that Jesus now serves as a Great High Priest, not only in having offered his body up for our salvation, but now as one who can sympathise with us our weaknesses and yet did not sin. He can help us overcome. He's been there, fully immersed in humanity in his human body. That should drive those of us who believe to approach God's throne of grace with confidence. Here is one who has faced similar difficulties, both external and internal – and succeeded! Through the various writers in the psalms we are pointed to someone who far beyond anyone else knows what it is to be stretched in his soul and put through his paces. By looking to Jesus as we read, we are led to him. Where we have not directly experienced such events listed in the psalms – and there are many we won't

– we should read them as the prayers of Christ, and prayers he prays *through* his body, the Church.

PRACTICAL RELEVANCE FOR LEADING

First, let us view the psalm as a song David wrote, understanding as much as we can about it. Although we don't know the exact circumstances of this particular psalm we can mull over David's struggle. He knew what it is to feel alone, and become depressed.

Second, without making ridiculous or trivial forward leaps, let us consider how it relates to some aspect of Christ's life, work, death or resurrection. Sometimes it's obvious. For example, just before his last breath on the cross, having already been brutally scourged, Jesus cried out, "My God, my God, why have you forsaken me?" (Matthew 27:46). This is a direct statement from Psalm 22. As the promised 'Son of David' (as Jesus is named in the very first sentence in the New Testament) he knows what it is to be isolated and abandoned, and in a most extreme form: crucifixion. The Bible teaches that Christ was abandoned on the cross by God. He had no human sympathy either. One of his disciples betrayed him and at his arrest they all deserted him and fled. One of his key leaders, Peter, later denied three times that he even knew him (Matthew 26:14-16, 34, 56). Plus, Jesus was within earshot. The whole geographical area where Jesus was crucified is described as descending into darkness in the hours leading up to his death.

Yet Christ trusted the God who could deliver him from death, from the grave. This was the glorious plan all along. This first line from one of David's other songs (Psalm 16) was fulfilled in Jesus and is quoted in the book of Acts. The Father did not permanently abandon his Son.

> *You will not abandon me to the realm of the dead, you will not let your holy one see decay.*
>
> **Acts 2:27**

Peter also preached that:

> *God raised him from the dead, freeing him from the agony of death, because it was impossible for death to keep its hold on him.*
>
> **Acts 2:24**

And he will deliver us too. In his last letter the apostle Paul included these words:

> *The Lord will rescue me from every evil attack and bring me safely into his heavenly kingdom.*
>
> **2 Timothy 4:18**

Early tradition states that he was beheaded in a Roman prison not long afterwards.[32] He was not kept from the sword at the end of his life any more than he was kept from beatings during it (Matthew 26:14-16, 34, 56). There is a final deliverance which awaits the believer. Death is not the Saviour, Christ is. And believers will also be raised bodily just as they have been raised spiritually (Ephesians 2, and 1 Corinthians 15).

Third, pray. Waiting and waiting for an answer from God, or seeking to feel close to God again can feel incredibly isolating. Perhaps you've been abandoned by someone at some point and it has led to depression. Perhaps it's taken years to diagnose, or years for you to realise. Sometimes we just don't know ourselves. God can sometimes use others to point out something. My wife can often see earlier than me how I'm really feeling; she can put her finger on something more quickly.

David knew what this felt like, and under divine inspiration (his words now form part of the Bible) wrote out his prayer, a prayer we can pray, a prayer of Christ. And having been completely abandoned on the cross, Christ now fully sympathises with anyone who not only feels but who may have actually *been* abandoned in their particular life circumstances.

---

32. For example, in Jewish historian Eusebius' *Ecclesiastical History*

Because he himself suffered when he was tempted, he is able to help those who are being tempted.

Hebrews 2:18

Because he is alive, Christ speaks directly to us through the psalm, drawing us to himself for encouragement, correction and strength. He's been there and he intercedes on our behalf.

Fourth, we can further apply the psalm to life and people. Anyone who has struggled with their own, or someone else's mental health, will recognise the unmistakable symptoms of depression in the psalm: continual sadness, mental torment, along with at times a great sense of hopelessness. Zest for life has departed, and in keeping with another symptom of depression the song-writer loses perspective. Here's David, a man of faith attributing characteristics to God that he would at all other times have found laughable, or only in the minds of his enemies with no faith whatsoever. Is this the same David we read about in the stories of his conquests elsewhere in the Bible? But that's just it, the story is not complete without these 'journal entries,' his prayers, his songs, his weaknesses and his sins. He's only human after all. Jesus experienced every human struggle there is. The psalms are instrumental for helping us navigate a vital relationship with Christ in the middle of even our darkest days.

A personal illustration

Many years ago after a couple of especially difficult events in life I found myself in a dark depression. I felt completely abandoned. It was not something I'd faced before. Even though my wife was fully aware of what was going on and was incredibly supportive, I just could not shake it off. I consulted a doctor, who spotted the symptoms right away and put me on medication lasting a few months. Being someone with faith I knew in my head that God does not abandon his children, but my circumstances and my feelings told me the opposite – every day. I had no personal pattern, and as far as I knew no family history of mental health problems, so it was an entirely new difficulty, a brand new enemy.

Mornings were the worst. Internally I was at times being thrown about by a torrent of emotion. Turmoil. It was like waking up inside some giant blender; at other times, a deep, dark pit. A few times I thought about ending it all, escape living. The fact that I knew exactly how I would do it told me I needed help, quickly. As well as seeing a doctor, an experienced Christian man good at helping others deal with such issues assisted me by offering regular counsel; I checked in with him every 2 or 3 months.

At times I scrawled down screaming, blunt notes to God. They described how utterly lost I felt. Abandoned. The word "Why?" appears regularly in my journals from that period. I even scribbled down a short poem I named, "Lost in Your Hands."

The Almighty Omniscient (All-Knowing) One forget? Impossible. Like the writer I was being irrational. But it's that loss of perspective, depression does that to you. If you've been there, or have a friend or partner who has, then you will know that you, or they, just can't 'snap out of it'. It took nearly two years to work through everything fully and come out the other end of the tunnel.

Some people end up living with depression for a long time, or experience intermittent periods of such depression their entire lives. A traumatic event in life can leave you with a wound that heals over time, but leaves you susceptible in that area. Some reading this will think that it's defeatism or a lack of faith, but the victory of faith is demonstrated by keeping going back to the One who knows what it is to feel utterly abandoned, sympathises with us, and who is willing to pour out grace to us direct from his heavenly throne.

Speak to yourself, don't just listen to yourself

At the end, the writer states that he will trust in God's unfailing love; it's another massive advantage of genuine Christian faith. Deep down most of us want to know that someone more powerful actually cares about us and can do something about it.

In other psalms, such as psalm 42 and 43, we see that David:

1. *Speaks to himself* – his own soul – in order to encourage himself in his faith.

2. He speaks *to himself about God* (God was still good, even if David felt completely forgotten).

3. Speaks *to God.*

There is self-discipline here: refusing to listen to our own 'self' with its dark thoughts, but speaking to our own soul and God instead. And in many Psalms the exact order may not matter. Sometimes David cried out directly to God with his first words. Isn't this normal when we are greatly troubled? Does a caring father whose child is distressed demand that they speak to him in some precise order each time? How much more then is the Lord of heaven and earth, who while Creator and Judge of the universe, like a caring father like no other. Indeed, all true fatherhood stems from him (Ephesians 3:14).

We'll revisit this matter of speaking to our own soul, and God, in the next chapter, because it's crucial in winning those battles that can go on inside our head and heart whether or not we face such extreme circumstances as David did.

It may sometimes feel easier to stay in bed and pull the sheets up, but our thoughts stay with us; they're inside our head and so going to bed won't solve anything unless we actually need to sleep. And the enemy of souls, Satan, loves to not only fire arrows of doubt and hate straight at our minds, he likes to 'stick the boot in,' i.e. kick us, when we're down.

For those in leadership, including those serving as church leaders, suffering in silence can be particularly difficult. Commenting on the suicide of a pastor, Ed Stetzer in the US writes, "Sometimes, the structure of the church itself creates and perpetuates that very curtain that keeps pastors from being in true relationships and getting the help they need."[33]

In some countries, admitting you're struggling with mental health issues, including depression and thoughts of suicide, has less stigma

---

33. https://www.christianitytoday.com/edstetzer/2019/september/pastor-dies-by-suicide-three-things-we-all-need-to-know.html Accessed September 2019

now than in past years. Some public figures have admitted their struggles; combined with the tragic suicide of others, it's brought the matter out into the open.

Get help from someone if you need it. I shared with you that I spoke with my wife, the doctor, and an experienced person good at counselling others; that's three different but entirely appropriate people. Some groups offer anonymity as people within it share how they are coping with depression or other mental health battles.

Leaders under pressure still need to express their emotions somehow, even if in private. I know someone who went off alone to 'have it out' with God when he discovered his partner had been murdered; what transpired in those hours of screaming and crying to the heavens God alone knows, but those tears are kept in a bottle (Psalm 56:8).

Say what you need to say

Speaking to your own soul, speaking to yourself about God, and speaking to God, not listening your own thoughts – these are absolutely key. You don't need many words unless you're a talker. The psalm that we read is around 100 words long when translated into English, but around half that length in the original language. That may be too much even for some. You may only have *one* sentence, or one word. It could also be something you've drawn or painted, you're just so numb from what's happened. That's one benefit, for example, of writing, singing (or creating) something based on how you feel. It forces you to artic-ulate or describe somehow what you are feeling. Other people find that going for a long walk or a run helps: you can talk to God as you go. Some might appreciate group counsel; for others it might not be so helpful.

Whatever, get those words out. Make psalm 13 your daily prayer. Meditate on it, chew on it like it's a piece of gum. Like I did at times you can also write out your own words, your own song or prayer. If you don't write much then talk to someone, build something, paint something, create something. You may even want to creatively destroy something like a plate or something else. The broken mess is just how you feel.

I was once helped with this when I was sitting in a church meeting one Sunday, miles away in my mind wrestling with some very dark thoughts. I was yanked back to the present when the preacher suddenly read out these words in the course of his message:

> *I am forgotten as though I were dead;*
> *I have become like broken pottery.*
>
> **Psalm 31:12**

At last! Someone who knew how I was feeling. I was no longer alone, and I had words to speak out. My feelings were validated. God had dealt with someone before who felt like a shattered vase. God could deal with me too. Sympathy – from heaven!

An old saying

There's an old French saying, 'Illness arrives on a horse and leaves on foot'. In other words, it typically arrives quickly but leaves gradually. David's inner battle seemed to be going on forever, and like some illness it seemed to be taking a long time to walk away. His mood was pitch black. We do not know the circumstances that caused David's struggle. I think the omission is deliberate, helpful. It means we can apply David's words to our own struggle, whatever it is. We can't say, "Ah, but I'm not in the same situation as him." Like him we may not *want* others to know the details of our difficulties, just that it's hard going. Some may not even care, let alone comprehend our inner battle. Yet in the psalms we see one, no two people – David *and* Christ – who know what it is to learn to fight, and win.

> *But I trust in your unfailing love; my heart rejoices in your*
> *salvation. I will sing the Lord's praise, for he has been good to me.*
>
> **Psalm 13:6**

TO SUMMARISE:

- If you are depressed, you are not alone; many people have wrestled with it, including some notable leaders.
- David knew what it was to be depressed and wrote about it in psalm 13.
- The psalms exist to point us to Christ who knows what it is to contend with such 'exercises for the soul' yet did not sin, *and now sympathises with us.*
- Christ prays for you; the psalm is his prayer.
- It does not have to end in permanent darkness.
- Learn to deal with depression by getting your words out somehow – why not use the psalm?
- Don't listen to your own thoughts, but in your praying and speaking, in any order:
  - Speak *to yourself*
  - Speak *to yourself about God*
  - Speak *to God*
- Speak to others who can help – that might be a doctor, pastor/elder, counsellor or support group, or perhaps a few of these.

QUESTIONS FOR REFLECTION OR DISCUSSION

1. Is the topic of depression or mental health talked about openly in your country? Why do you think that is?

2. Who do you know that has struggled with the same dark thoughts like David was having? How have you tended to view that person, or depression itself? (something just for weak people?)

3. Are you struggling with depression? You can take some tests online to see, but seeing a doctor is by far the best idea. Some medication can also give us the breathing space to slowly get perspective.

4. If you do discover or know for sure that you are definitely struggling with depression, then use a few words to write down or speak out exactly how you feel: talk *to yourself*, talk to yourself *about* God, and talk *to* God. Use psalm 13. You may wish to draw something instead, speak to someone, join some sort of group that might help; or create something that reflects how you feel, that helps you give shape to your words and your thoughts.

5. Is there anyone you know who is really wrestling with dark thoughts? They may be more on the edge of life than you realise. In some cases that may entail asking them how they were going to commit suicide, and if possible, removing that method or opportunity (it will also entail some aftercare since removing the item does not get to the root of the problem).

6. There are 150 psalms. Why not read one a day for the next 150 days? As so many others find, you may discover the timing remarkable as your life events and those of the psalm intersect. And slowly the possibility of a growing and genuine faith begins to dawn as you look to the Saviour to whom these songs and prayers ultimately point.

CHAPTER

9

WHEN THE TANK IS EMPTY

A NUMBER OF YEARS ago I was chatting with a young church leader in his 20s. He was clearly on the brink when he asked me privately during a family BBQ we were attending: "Do you ever feel like going off and sinning really badly?" This wasn't the kind of sauce I was expecting with my burger, but he clearly needed someone to talk to, even a stranger who he sensed might be able to sympathise with him. He was on the edge and felt like drowning his sorrows in some vice or other.

None of us is immune to finding solace in the wrong places, in the wrong habits. Some of us may have also experienced something more dramatic, and it can happen when we are running on empty.

It shows itself in anything from totally irrational or hasty decisions, losing your temper with someone, collapsing in an emotional heap, or running away. It's when as a leader you've been burning too much midnight oil; taken one too many words of criticism; felt too heavily the expectations of self or others; taken on too much responsibility; not delegated effectively, or in some cases not at all; seen one too many people; done everything right, but feel overcome by the pressure; or are now facing some unexpected and tragic turn of events. It's when you have reached the end of the line, when there's nothing left in the tank. Just what do you do in such a place?

Since this recorded episode in David's life is fairly long, for this chapter I've broken it into sections and laced together the four steps outlined at the start of the book: background, David's response and the flaws we see, God's provision at the time and how it points us to Christ, and how leaders can apply this as they look to the Lord.

CALLING ON GOD DURING A GREAT CRISIS

David now understood what this was like. There was a day, a moment, indeed a *place* where he reached his limit. Apart from the murders of his sons Amnon and especially Absalom, an outworking of God's judgement on David's own sin in murdering Uriah after taking his wife Bathsheba (2 Samuel 12:10 – 18:33), what you are about to read (or listen to) is probably the lowest point in David's life. He would not forget the place or the occasion, and it would go down in battle history (which it has, you're about to listen to it or read it). He was not quite 30 years of age.

Attempting to somehow get his way back into Israel, David managed to persuade a local Philistine ruler, Achish, in whose district he had temporarily taken refuge from King Saul, to let him join the ranks of the Philistines at the rear. His idea backfired. Let's read or listen again to the narrative.

> *The Philistines gathered all their forces at Aphek, and Israel camped by the spring in Jezreel. As the Philistine rulers marched with their units of hundreds and thousands, David and his men were marching at the rear with Achish. The commanders of the Philistines asked, "What about these Hebrews?"*
>
> *Achish replied, "Is this not David, who was an officer of Saul king of Israel? He has already been with me for over a year, and from the day he left Saul until now, I have found no fault in him."*
>
> *But the Philistine commanders were angry with Achish and said, "Send the man back, that he may return to the place you assigned him. He must not go with us into battle, or he will turn against us*

during the fighting. How better could he regain his master's favor than by taking the heads of our own men? Isn't this the David they sang about in their dances:

"'Saul has slain his thousands,

and David his tens of thousands'?"

So Achish called David and said to him, "As surely as the Lord lives, you have been reliable, and I would be pleased to have you serve with me in the army. From the day you came to me until today, I have found no fault in you, but the rulers don't approve of you. Now turn back and go in peace; do nothing to displease the Philistine rulers."

"But what have I done?" asked David. "What have you found against your servant from the day I came to you until now? Why can't I go and fight against the enemies of my lord the king?"

Achish answered, "I know that you have been as pleasing in my eyes as an angel of God; nevertheless, the Philistine commanders have said, 'He must not go up with us into battle.' Now get up early, along with your master's servants who have come with you, and leave in the morning as soon as it is light."

So David and his men got up early in the morning to go back to the land of the Philistines, and the Philistines went up to Jezreel.

1 Samuel 29

Having tried to slip in at the back with the advancing Philistine army about to face the Israelites – David's own people – David and his men were sent home. It's little wonder that the Philistine commanders were infuriated with King Achish of Gath, one of their main towns (and, interestingly, also Goliath's hometown).

It was a lengthy march back to base for David and his men with all their supplies – around 50 miles, likely a three-day march. On their return they were met with a devastating sight. Perhaps a trail of smoke ahead on the horizon told them something had gone terribly wrong. The text doesn't say, but you can imagine them running the last stretch.

> *David and his men reached Ziklag on the third day. Now the Amalekites had raided the Negev and Ziklag. They had attacked Ziklag and burned it, and had taken captive the women and everyone else in it, both young and old. They killed none of them, but carried them off as they went on their way.*
>
> *When David and his men reached Ziklag, they found it destroyed by fire and their wives and sons and daughters taken captive. So David and his men wept aloud until they had no strength left to weep. David's two wives had been captured—Ahinoam of Jezreel and Abigail, the widow of Nabal of Carmel. David was greatly distressed because the men were talking of stoning him; each one was bitter in spirit because of his sons and daughters.*

1 Samuel 30:1-6a

David and his men found their homes ransacked, burned, and everyone missing. Ziklag was their temporary base, not some modern day FOB (forward operating base) with their spouses and children secure and far away back in their home country. Their families were missing. Talk about a crisis, especially for David the commander.

He and his men wept until they were spent – no emotional or physical energy left. Except for those in the military, very few of us can relate to such an exacting physical and emotional toll. (Some women who have had a long and difficult labour might disagree!) You've just marched for three days in the direction of where the battle's going to be, only to be sent back. That's a hundred miles over six days. With your kit. Can you imagine coming back dog-tired to find your base burned to the ground and everyone's wife and children missing, *including yours?* Unimaginably distressful.

David's men turned on him, talked about stoning him. What had they got to lose? They'd lost everything else, and he was their main leader. They felt like sinning really badly and drowning their sorrows, not in alcohol or some other vice like my friend at that communal BBQ I mentioned at the start, but in David's blood.

David's best friend, Jonathan, was not around to encourage him as before. Samuel was long dead. What should he do? Blame his men?

Blame someone else? Blame his commanding officer. (But that was him!) Blame God? Run away? Some people in such extreme situations do indeed run away, abandon ship, and leave others to sink or swim. No mentor, old friend, peer, pastor, priest or counsellor; nothing but tiredness, great anguish over his family and the response of his broken men.

What *is* recorded for us is not only David's level of stress (it says he was '*greatly* distressed' because there was talk of stoning him) but how he responded. It showed what he was made of deep down, how he would respond as before when under great pressure. Tough circumstances don't just build character, they reveal it.

> *But David found strength in the Lord his God.*
>
> *Then David said to Abiathar the priest, the son of Ahimelek, "Bring me the ephod." Abiathar brought it to him, and David inquired of the Lord, "Shall I pursue this raiding party? Will I overtake them?"*
>
> *"Pursue them," he answered. "You will certainly overtake them and succeed in the rescue."*
>
> **1 Samuel 30:6b-8**

HOW DAVID RESPONDED AND HOW GOD PROVIDED FOR HIM

It says that David 'encouraged himself in the Lord,' literally 'strengthened himself in the Lord.' This was no token gesture or religious platitude to help him cope as he was about to go into battle. It was everything. His faith was everything, and it kicked into gear bigtime. Again.

David strengthened himself in the Lord. God provided strength.

'What on earth does that look like?' you might ask.

It was not merely some form of self-help or self administered psychotherapy (whatever branch), food or anything else. He strengthened himself, though with one massive difference: *in the Lord his God*. This is where, in whom, he found strength: not in himself, not his faith, but God, his God. Given how some of his songs and prayers are laid out, it could have involved several things. We touched on this in the previous chapter. Let me suggest to you that as well as calling on God (in other words, speaking *to* God) it may have involved speaking to himself, and speaking to himself about God.

Let's break those three things down further. Here's an example of speaking to your own soul from that song that David wrote that we looked at briefly in the last chapter:

> *Why, my soul, are you downcast?*
> *Why so disturbed within me?*
>
> **Psalm 42:5a**

First, we see how he first addresses himself, his own soul. We also see it Psalm 57:8:

> *Awake, my soul! Awake, harp and lyre!*

It is very easy to listen to your own thoughts of panic or pain or defeat or sin when things are hard. But David *talked* to himself, spoke to own soul, encouraged himself. This can help us get perspective. He did not remind himself of how great he was or of how much of a champion he was. Nor did he 'think positively.' Such methods, while certainly better than thinking negatively, simply will not cut it in these sort of circumstances. What's more, secular self-help ideas or advice do not direct us to God for strengthening, only self. In that sense they are in complete opposition to the gospel of grace that declares that we are nothing without Christ, yet complete *in him* (Colossians 2:10).[34] Let us look to the Lord and our identity *in him* as beloved children of God (1 John 3:1), not *inside* of ourselves.

An old lie in new clothes

It's one of the fattest and yet actually the oldest lie around that has crept into some strands of Christian teaching: look within yourself

---

34. Sinner yet saint. Reformer Martin Luther framed it: *simul justus et peccator* (simultaneously justified as a saint, yet still a sinner).

(Genesis 3:5).[35] After all, aren't we gods? Can't we be like God? Aren't we 'little gods'? Not in the sense some argue. When Jesus said 'you are gods' (John 10:34) he meant in the sense of God's representatives, God's image-bearers on earth; not on a par with God, or little gods. (It's also why believers are called kings and priests – Revelation 1:6; 1 Peter 2:9.) In context, Jesus was defending his divinity. He was rightly referring to *himself*, i.e. if you who are here on earth can be called 'gods' in the sense of divine representatives, how much more *God the Son*. He was not blaspheming; it's who he is. We mortals are not gods in the sense of being God or a god. Nor should a Christian view themselves as some sort of 50% saint-and-sinner half-breed. We are beloved children, princes and princesses, priests of the Most High God. And that by virtue of Christ's victory on the cross as we are trying to make clear in this book.

So David did not listen to himself or the anxious and angry voices around. He spoke to himself, his own soul.

Second, he also talked to himself *about God*, telling himself to put his hope in God, reminding himself of *where* he needed to put his trust.

Put your hope in God,
for I will yet praise him,
my Saviour and my God.
Psalm 42:5b

We also see it in the very first line of Psalm 103:

Praise the Lord, my soul.

Do you see how he's speaking to himself, his soul, and directing it to God?

Third, he then talked *to* God.

---

35. The devil's half-truth to Eve that she could be like God. She and Adam were made in the *image* of God.

I say to God my Rock,
"Why have you forgotten me?
Why must I go about mourning,
oppressed by the enemy."
Psalm 42:9

Note the brutal honesty. God is still his Rock, even when it doesn't feel like it or look like it. David's act of 'strengthening himself in the Lord' at Ziklag may have lasted only a few minutes, we don't know. I highly doubt that his men would have let him go off for the whole afternoon or the evening to collect his thoughts.

As I've mentioned before, as we see in the psalms the exact order of speaking to self, speaking to God, and speaking to ourselves about God doesn't really matter. What matters is that we actually *do it*.

Writing, walking

I recall one cloudy afternoon pulling into a café after work when my mind began to become filled with terrible, black thoughts. I was in a very difficult situation at work. So I found a corner seat, sat down and wrote some words to myself, to myself about God, and then to God. Put together it went something like this (I've summarised it a little):

Fraser, it's OK, this is a very difficult time for you, but it's not the end of the line. It feels like it, but it's not.

God has work for you to do. He has a work for you to do. He has your back. And has he not promised to be with you forever? Hasn't he spoken to you in the past very clearly? Yes, he has. He's promised in Scripture. Remember how he spoke to you before. How he provided for you and your wife. Remember that time? (in my journal I jot down some details). Yes, he is with you and for you.

(And then a prayer) 'Father, you have said you'd never leave or forsake me. You've given me everlasting life through your Son, Jesus. Thank you. You've also spoke clearly to me about my future.

Take note of my distress! Fulfil your gracious word. What you've promised you will fulfil. Hear my cry, and lift me up I pray! Thank you that you hear me. Amen.'

The whole process took about half an hour, and I filled out one page in my small journal – a notebook. It was intense, focused. I didn't look up the entire time except to try and think of the right words to sum how I felt, what I wanted to say. At the start it felt a little mechanical, but the words soon came out. I could have as easily said them out loud somewhere in private, but given it would have involved, as it has at other times, looking heavenwards and shouting or crying out, the café was more suitable as a place to write. And you know what? My feelings of anguish lifted as quickly as they had arrived. I was astonished and I actually re-opened my journal again to write down the effect of what had just occurred in my soul. And here's the thing: My circumstances had not changed one bit, and neither did they for some considerable time. But I'd won an important battle and strengthened myself in the Lord my God. And at times I have had to keep doing it.

I remember another time going for a long walk near a harbour, crying out in my distress for God to speak a word of comfort over a certain matter. As I continued walking my attention was drawn to two people in a small boat. I heard no audible voice but clearly sensed the Lord impress on me that I was to stop and watch. I couldn't hear the people on the boat because they were too far away, but I could tell from their movements that one was instructing the other about how the boat worked, how the sails operated, etc. The very clear sense I received at the moment from the Lord was that he was teaching me things during this season that I didn't fully understand, but out on the high seas, with the wind blowing strongly later, I would appreciate the lessons I was now being given. Peace descended on me like a large blanket. I received strength to carry on, to obey God in what he had given me to do at that time. I had taken the matter to the Lord and strengthened myself in the Lord my God. God provided the strength.

Preparation

Can we prepare for times when there may be nothing left in the tank, perhaps when we're all alone, or feeling all alone despite there being other people around in whatever crisis we may be facing? I'd say 'Yes'.

Soldiers in training are put through the necessary preparation. In his book *Mud, Sweat and Tears,* Bear Grylls recalls how in the selection process for joining the British SAS he often felt like he had nothing left in the tank after many miles of back-breaking marches carrying hefty backpacks over Welsh mountains. He had to dig deep. "Come on Bear, finish this thing" he would often *say to himself.* He might also recall a Bible verse he knew (in other words *he spoke to himself about God*), and if there was a fellow soldier nearby, they would assist each other with similar encouraging words. It's also why elite soldiers are put through stern tests, including simulated capture and interrogation.

OTHER WAYS GOD PROVIDED

Notably, David also got advice from the priest. Not for the first time…he did it when Saul was hunting him down (2 Samuel 23:9). Despite the extremity of the situation David did not charge ahead recklessly but first consulted the Almighty through this key means he had available. Again, this is in contrast to his predecessor Saul, who rebelled against God by failing to wait for direction before acting, or blatantly ignoring prior and clear instructions. It would have involved what's called in Hebrew the Urim and the Thummin held by the priest, two stones used to casts lots to determine if the will of God was 'Yes' or 'No'. It's how God gave David that double answer: Yes, and Yes. Two questions, two answers. Another translation has it: you *shall surely overtake,* and you *shall surely rescue* (ESV). In the original the word translated 'rescue' or 'recover' or 'deliver' is repeated. God had definitely determined that David *would* succeed, as exhausted as he and his men were. Can you imagine David falling to his knees and lifting his hands and head up to the heavens and thanking God?

After hearing God's clear double-answer, David kept going with the other men who could perhaps find something in their reserve tank – around two thirds of his growing battalion of men. As we'll see in the next chapter, David still had a long way to go.

CHRIST THE GREAT HIGH PRIEST AND ONE WHO WAS STRENGTHENED AS HE EMPTIED HIMSELF

The New Testament declares that we all have access to one Great High Priest who is able to save us completely, for he lives forever (unlike Abiathar the priest David enquired through) and he lives forever to intercede for us (Hebrews 7:25). There is only one mediator between men and women and God (1 Timothy 2:5) and he is more than willing to show us what to do. No casting of lots required, yet note the devotion to the Lord whether using lots or not. It's as you and I give ourselves completely over to the Lord that we are able to discern his good, pleasing and perfect will (Romans 12:1-3). If we never have a sense of God's will for us, it may be because we are not fully surrendered: we've haven't really put our lives on the altar.

Jesus also knows what it is to be emptied but never give up or give in. We only have to consider some of the more distressing moments in his earthly life to see this. For example, under immense pressure to give up after 40 days without food in a desert, he fended off direct and personal temptation from the devil himself (Luke 4). On the night of his trial, Jesus' friends abandoned him before he was beaten, flogged and then crucified early the following morning. Such was the agony Jesus felt in those hours prior to his arrest that he prayed passionately for the 'cup of suffering' he was about to drink to be taken away. The extremity of the situation made him sweat as if it were drops of blood. As with his temptation in the desert, it's one of the times where it is recorded that an angel came and strengthened him (Luke 22:42). In his humanity, Christ the God-man needed an angel. In his human weakness he wanted the cup of suffering to pass, but he did not give up, praying, "Not my will but yours be done" (Luke 23:42). He had a task to complete. In his very last breath on the cross he cried, "It is finished." Christ was emptied so that we could be filled up.

This sense of emptying is conveyed in what many commentators regard as an early Christian hymn or song in Paul's letter to the Philippians. As he appealed to his readers and listeners to have the same mindset as Christ and look out for each others' interests, Paul wrote:

Who, being in very nature God,
did not consider equality with God something to be used to his
own advantage;
*rather, he **made himself nothing***
by taking the very nature of a servant,
being made in human likeness.
And being found in appearance as a man,
he humbled himself
by becoming obedient to death—
even death on a cross!
Therefore God exalted him to the highest place
and gave him the name that is above every name, that at the name
of Jesus every knee should bow,
in heaven and on earth and under the earth,
and every tongue acknowledge that Jesus Christ is Lord,
to the glory of God the Father.

Philippians 2:5-11 (emboldened words mine)

The phrase 'he emptied himself' literally means he 'emptied [himself] out'. Since Christ is God, this is best understood as meaning that he laid aside *independent* use of his divine powers and clothed himself in human flesh. The incarnation, *in carne* (in meat), God became embodied *in flesh*. Here's perhaps a helpful illustration: If a King or Queen laid aside independent use of their powers and got dressed in cheap clothes and mixed among people, would they for that reason cease to be the King or the Queen? No. They've just, as it were, emptied themselves, become like one of us. What's more, Jesus took on the very nature of a servant. 'I am among you as one who serves' he said (Luke 22:27).

PRACTICAL RELEVANCE FOR LEADING

Under extreme pressure we more readily accept our limitations and throw ourselves on God. You may feel like throwing yourself on God for the very first time, some crisis may have brought you to your knees. It is why so many people look heavenward and find faith during some sort of distressing situation. The Holy Spirit can use such occasions to convict sinners of their desperate need of divine assistance: we more fully realise that we actually *can't* do it on our own. God must be our all in all, our everything.

If you're someone with a living faith,[36] here are some practical measures that will help you develop emotional and spiritual resilience, strengthening yourself in the Lord. As you can see, each of them can be put into one of three categories that we've mentioned before – speak to yourself, to yourself about God, and speak directly to God.

Here they are:

- Recount the faithfulness of God in the past.
- Recall what the Bible says about who God is (David called him his 'Rock').
- Remind yourself about how God called you to your leadership task.
- Recount how God specifically guided you in the past.
- Sift through any encouraging messages you've received from others before (which is also why encouraging others is so important as they can look back over your message). Keeping them in a folder (digital or otherwise) is a good idea.
- Journal out or speak out your thoughts and prayers; writing or speaking out what's going on forces us to choose our words, to think about what we want to say.

Also:

- If believing friends are available, lean on them. Some years earlier, Jonathan travelled to see David and helped him find

---

36. It's possible to have a *dead* faith! Like the devil. See James 2:14-26, especially the last verse.

strength in the Lord (2 Samuel 23:16). I've no doubt that will have involved reminding David of God's promises to him, about what God felt about him, and what Jonathan felt about David – they had history.

- Meet regularly with a mentor if you have one; if not, ask someone more experienced you respect if they would mentor and disciple you. On another occasion David went and stayed with the prophet Samuel at Ramah, probably the safest place for him (1 Samuel 19:18).

Learning to encourage ourselves in the Lord is a mark of maturity that will help us learn how to stand on our own two feet, spiritually speaking. The side benefit is that it helps with our emotional health as well. It cannot fail to because we are body, soul and spirit – they are interlinked. God wants to sanctify us completely, our whole being, which is the sense of 1 Thessalonians 5:23. And we really only develop this godly habit when we're down. As one old, battle-hardened Scottish preacher said to a greatly discouraged man sitting in the congregation, 'Son, you don't grow fruit on the mountaintops, you grow it in the valleys.' It's the fruit of daily choices we make when the tank is half-full. So don't listen to yourself, your own thoughts: talk *to yourself*, talk *to yourself about* God, and *talk to God*. Develop that three-fold habit, so when things unsettle you and you begin *listening* to yourself and all your anxious, fearful (or angry) thoughts, then the discipline will kick in and you will know what to do. This godly habit will help you respond in similar fashion when things are harder; or perhaps, as in David's case, critical.

Start now

The broader story about David shows that he made consistently good choices over the years before this episode. Such ingrained habits for him also included worshipping God when no one was looking, obeying his father in sheep-rearing, consistently refusing to take revenge against Saul the king even though he had several opportunities to do so, faithfully exercising leadership of others, consulting Abiathar the priest, and listening to others such as Abigail who stopped him en route to killing Nabal and all the men in his family. David spoke to his soul and to God through it all.

Character is crucial in holding us up when the pressure is really on. Your tank may not be empty now, but half full. So start now and build character by learning to encourage yourself in the Lord. It will help when there's nothing left in the tank.

QUESTIONS FOR REFLECTION OR DISCUSSION

1. What stood out for you as you read the biblical story?

2. Recall a time when you sense God supported you in the middle of an especially difficult time. How *specifically* did you find strength in God?

3. If you are an older mentor, share with those who are younger one story of someone you know (it might be yourself) who kept going during a difficult event or season. How did you lean on God? What did God do?

4. What do you think about this idea of learning not to listen to yourself, but instead talking to yourself, talking to yourself about God, and talking *to* God. Share your thoughts with others in the group if you're in one.

5. What specific, practical steps are you going to take to put this into practice whenever you start to listen to your own thoughts?

6. Consider Christ and how he emptied himself for you and me. Ponder *him*. It's the best strengthening agent there is !

CHAPTER

10

GLORY AND GIVING

W E NOW READ of a remarkable turnaround. God's promise strengthens David's faith and he gets moving. Nothing quite like answered prayer! The men were exhausted but victorious. Yet among them were some who caused David problems. Their attitude stands in contrast to David's. We continue the story starting at 1 Samuel 30:9 through to the end of the chapter.

David and the six hundred men with him came to the Besor Valley, where some stayed behind. Two hundred of them were too exhausted to cross the valley, but David and the other four hundred continued the pursuit.

They found an Egyptian in a field and brought him to David. They gave him water to drink and food to eat — part of a cake of pressed figs and two cakes of raisins. He ate and was revived, for he had not eaten any food or drunk any water for three days and three nights.

David asked him, "Who do you belong to? Where do you come from?"

He said, "I am an Egyptian, the slave of an Amalekite. My master abandoned me when I became ill three days ago. We raided the Negev of the Kerethites, some territory belonging to Judah and the Negev of Caleb. And we burned Ziklag."

David asked him, "Can you lead me down to this raiding party?"

He answered, "Swear to me before God that you will not kill me or hand me over to my master, and I will take you down to them."

*He led David down, and there they were, scattered over the countryside, eating, drinking and reveling because of the great amount of plunder they had taken from the land of the Philistines and from Judah. David fought them from dusk until the evening of the next day, and none of them got away, except four hundred young men who rode off on camels and fled. David recovered everything the Amalekites had taken, including his two wives. Nothing was missing: young or old, boy or girl, **plunder** or anything else they had taken. David **brought everything back.***

*He took all the flocks and herds, and his men drove them ahead of the other livestock, saying, "This is David's **plunder**."*

*Then David came to the two hundred men who had been too exhausted to follow him and who were left behind at the Besor Valley. They came out to meet David and the men with him. As David and his men approached, he asked them how they were. But all the evil men and troublemakers among David's followers said, "Because they did not go out with us, we will not share with them the **plunder** we recovered. However, each man may take his wife and children and go."*

*David replied, "No, my brothers, you must not do that with what **the Lord** has given us. **He** has protected us and delivered into our hands the raiding party that came against us. Who will listen to what you say? The share of the man who stayed with the supplies is to be the same as that of him who went down to the battle. All will share alike." David made this a statute and ordinance for Israel from that day to this.*

*When David reached Ziklag, he sent some of the **plunder** to the elders of Judah, who were his friends, saying, "Here is a gift for you from the **plunder of the Lord's enemies.***"

*David sent **it (i.e. some of the plunder)** to those who were in*

Bethel, Ramoth Negev and Jattir; to those in Aroer, Siphmoth, Eshtemoa and Rakal; to those in the towns of the Jerahmeelites and the Kenites; to those in Hormah, Bor Ashan, Athak and Hebron; and to those in all the other places where he and his men had roamed."

1 Samuel 30:9-31 (emboldened words and inserts mine)

DAVID'S PERCEPTION AND PRECEDENT

Fighting throughout the night and all through the next day, David and his men won through, claimed the spoils, and got their families back. It was a long, hard battle. The ensuing fight would have involved intense periods of combat as well as lulls in the battle as David's men slowly pushed through the enemy camp. No one can fight non-stop during a 24-hour firefight, certainly not after what they had just experienced: a 100-mile march over several days before facing the nightmare scenario of finding your loved ones missing.

David set a precedent after the event. It was not fear or unwillingness that prevented the two hundred from continuing, just sheer exhaustion. One extra reward for the four hundred was that they got to fight it out at the end. They were there, and would for the rest of their lives be able to tell it to their children and grandchildren; they were among those who had kept going. Any proper soldier will tell you that they would want to take part in the fight if and when it took place.

The fact that you need people back at base or in a supporting role is also no different from the military today. Many others need to stay back and look after the supplies or keep the supplies coming in (logistics). For every soldier on the front there are many more personnel behind the scenes.

At root, David appreciated that *God* had given them the victory. His conviction that all should share in the plunder took him right back to his desperate prayer and God's answer that he would definitely succeed. God was to get the glory. Little prayer will typically lead to little glory, for we haven't asked the Almighty what he feels about a situation or sought him for an answer. But when we hear his answer or have at least sensed, know deep down that he has heard us, we can be at peace whatever it is. For David it was a very important moment. From the depths of despair to the worn-out heights of a hard-won victory.

Just pause and consider the sweep of emotions, the hugs there would have between the men and their families. Such great relief! (We're not told all that the women and children suffered other than their abduction as it's not the point of the story.)

GOD'S GRACE THEN AND HOW IT POINTS TO CHRIST

David and his men *recovered* or *rescued* or *delivered* everything and everyone – they brought everything back. The same word in Hebrew (*natsal* means to deliver or snatch or plunder) and it's used twice in verse 8, twice in verse 18, and again we have it in verse 22 in the original (*italics* below). Depending on the context and translation, in English it's 'recover' or 'rescue' or 'deliver'. Let's read or listen to the relevant verses in English again:

> ...you shall surely *recover* (everything) *without fail.*
>
> ...David *recovered* everything....and David *rescued* his wives.
>
> ...the plunder we *recovered.*

It's the same word used in Scripture to declare that God had come down to *rescue* the Israelites from slavery in Egypt (Exodus 3:8). And it's the same word David used when he boldly exclaimed before Saul that the Lord who *delivered* him from the paw of lions and bears would also *deliver* him from the hand of Goliath. Same faith, same God, different situation (1 Sam 17:37). And to reinforce this the narrator adds: nothing was missing...David brought everything back (verse 19). It was a complete restoration.

The Lord gave them victory, and plenty *plunder* – a word that appears many times as well. They called it 'David's plunder'. Yet he knew it wasn't him who brought it about. As he declared to Goliath: It's not by sword or spear that the Lord saves; for the battle is the Lord's

(1 Sam 17:47). Again, same faith, same God, different enemy. After all, how can a mere human being take on a bear, or a 9-foot man, or a much bigger army when yours is depleted and exhausted?

Not only did he insist all shared in it, he sent some to his friends back in Judah. A smart political move but also evidence of what he felt about the spoils they had gained. It was a time for celebration; for sharing, not stinginess. That ought to speak a word to us. The spoils of victory should be shared by all; those more capable should not take the lion's share leaving little or nothing for the others. It's different if someone is lazy. As the Scripture says, "If a man shall not work, he shall not eat" (2 Thessalonians 3:10).

By way of analogy, the most magnificent aspect of this great reversal of fortunes, from despair to winning, should lift our eyes to the fantastic deliverer Jesus. As with the defeat of Goliath when they were up against it, David's leadership and victory points us to the One who can rescue all, deliver all, bring everything back. He is the restorer of our souls. Just as God the Father brought back from the dead our Lord Jesus, the Shepherd and overseer of our souls (Hebrews 13:20), so too can the Saviour rescue and bring back the plunder. The enemy Satan comes to steal, kill and destroy (John 10) but the Rescuer came to give life, to restore. It is his plunder. We are his. And like the godly soldiers (not the troublemakers I hope!) who joined David's ranks and recognised him as the true anointed one, supporting him in his role as future king (see 1 Chronicles 12 and 11:10), let us also follow after our great Saviour and Rescuer, lifting our swords (the Scriptures) and our voices (our prayers) *with him*. He is the one who delivered us, and he is the one who can bring everything back.

When Jesus was accused by the teachers of the law of being possessed by a demon he included in his reply, "...no one can enter a strong man's house without first tying him up. Then he can plunder the strong man's house" (Matthew 12:22-29). Via the cross Jesus has defeated the enemy, but that needs enforcing on a practical level. The enemy is stubborn and can even gain a foothold in the life of a believer through their disobedience. So just as David led his men into battle to recover the plunder, so the Lord leads his people in prayer which can at times include binding the enemy (Matthew 16:19). This is one privilege involved in the fight of intercessory prayer. As we pray with others, we may sense God has given us permission to move against some spirit or other which is hindering or afflicting a person or a group of people. We see practical examples of this when Jesus freed a woman who had been sick due to an evil spirit, and when Paul cast out a demon of a fortune-telling girl, an evil spirit of divination (Luke 13; Acts 16).

Isn't all this evidence of the kingdom coming in power? Of the anointed one recovering what has been stolen by the enemy? Let us seek him in prayer as the Rescuer, pleading with him for any loved ones taken captive, for those who were in our care that the enemy has got hold of, perhaps dragged away.

In intercession it always begins with God, not the evil one. And let us also share the plunder, the good things, the joy of restoration and deliverance as we see God answering our prayers. He is the Victor and the Anointed One, the King and Rescuer who was, who is, and who is to come.

PRACTICAL RELEVANCE

1. If you already lead in some capacity (which could be as simple as leading your own family or a small group of believers), and you sense the Lord leading to move on or move out of something, after consulting with others *do so*. We see an example of this with Saul and Barnabas when they were set apart for the work God had called them to do. It's a good example of people praying together and sensing the Lord's mind on a matter (Acts 13). This may or may not include a word of prophecy or a word of wisdom shared at the meeting, but it will certainly involve discussing as well as praying what we sense the Holy Spirit is saying on a matter.

2. Take others with you, having compassion on those who can't keep going. Is there another role they could take up in support of those in more forward positions? Both are needed.

Sidenote on Church leadership

Something worth repeating as we consider leadership and sharing what God has provided. I mentioned something about this in the introduction. Church leaders need to be aware of not acting like kings like David was becoming where he only consulted with God via the priest, the Law, and heeded the words of the prophets. He would also have advisers later, but he was the still the king, the chief.

In the New Testament, solo leadership or a one-man band in an established local church in which other leaders rubber stamp decisions by one senior leader is simply not biblical; neither is a two-tier eldership where one or more leaders call the shots. At the pioneering stage where no eldership is established, one person may tend to hear God more clearly on the direction they should go, but even then teamwork still matters. For example, where Paul had a vision about 'the man from Macedonia' it reads that '...*we* got ready...concluding that God had called *us*' (Acts 16:10). Once a plurality of elders is appointed it's a team of equals, even though they will not be equally gifted. Some will be more prominent than others just as we see with Peter, James and John among the Twelve (apostles). But an elder is an elder is an elder. All elders, paid or unpaid, are equally called even if not equally gifted. Equality with diversity.

Local church leaders (and I'm using the term here to mean elders/pastors – it's the same thing/role, see footnote)[37] are also not above

---

37. Three different words are used for 'elders' (v17), 'overseers' (v28) and 'to pastor' [verb], i.e. to shepherd or care for, by Paul when he says his final words to the Ephesian elders, a single group of men (Acts 20:18-35). And in his first letter, Peter used the same word for 'shepherd' as Paul does when addressing or speaking about elders, i.e. pastors (1 Peter 5:1 and Ephesians 4:11). In other words, elders and pastors are one-in-the-same: they are *not* two different classes of people. It is the same with ministers and elders, pastors and elders, or senior pastor and elders, or any other kind of separation, whatever names are used. Therefore, a board of elders that does no shepherding but hires paid staff pastors to do it is not a biblical leadership; it has more in common with the governance structure of a charity where a Board of Trustees has nothing to do with the executive functions, i.e. the running of the organisation, but instead recruits staff to do it [entirely correct *in that context*]. This is a major misunderstanding in some churches, with practical ramifications. The reason elders and deacons are not mentioned in every letter as with Philippians (1:1), is that Paul etc were writing to local churches as local bodies. The message was for the whole body, just as someone preaching as a guest would address the whole fellowship as a priority, not simply leaders behind the scenes, as important as that is as part of encouraging and equipping local churches.

being questioned. Indeed, in the context of the local church, elders, just like deacons, must *first* be tested (1 Timothy 3:10 ('also' – ESV), which isn't something consistent with any resulting autocratic leadership style or where people swear undying loyalty to a single leader and his vision. Leaders must lead, but there's a gentleness to this, one which speaks *to* and *with* the flock, consulting with them; not charging ahead as one who considers those looking to them know nothing. After all, they have direct access to the King of Heaven too. So if your gift is to lead, lead as part of a team. If you don't have a team, then disciple others who will learn to lead alongside you, and with you. It's telling when you consider the leadership of more dominant, noted individuals: many of them don't tend to do peers well, being unable or unwilling to see strong leaders develop and walk alongside them, even those who do not possess a public preaching gift. Let's remember that it's the Holy Spirit who appoints overseers, elders (Acts 20:28). In that sense elders are recognised more than appointed. Which is why the testing process matters: people in general can help affirm a person's call, not just any senior figure. As well as giving younger leaders responsibility as part of mentoring them, one recommendation is to have an open forum for any prospective elders to answer questions from the congregation (or part of it) over doctrinal matters, e.g. when asked, can they open their Bible and point to Scriptures and defend the deity of Christ and other key doctrines? This is especially important in testing their ability to teach since most of them will *not* doing that publicly (but in small groups or within homes – 1 Timothy 5:17).

If we view Timothy not as an 'ordained minister' or 'senior pastor' but more a 'man on the move', i.e. an itinerant servant or apostolic delegate, who like Titus is ready to go where someone with an apostolic mantle sent them, then the importance of a fully functioning eldership becomes more clear. Titus 3:13 makes it clear that leaders like Timothy and Titus were not local pastors. 1 and 2 Timothy are nowhere in Scripture called the 'pastoral epistles' or 'pastorals' – that's a phrase coined by a scholar called Berdot in 1703. 1 and 2 Timothy aren't really a pastor's or a minister's handbook. The two letters were written to a young itinerant leader who like Titus was to set things straight, sort out doctrine (the main reason was Timothy told to remain in Ephesus – 1 Tim 1:3), do the work of an evangelist, *and then move on, letting the local elders (as a body) lead*, but remaining in touch and praying for them, just like Paul did.

3. If you sense after seeking God, that he is with those leading you, and that what they are proposing is the will of God and that they are not leading the flock or organisation down some rabbit trail or false path, then follow. Hebrews 13:17 states 'Obey your leaders'. As per my comments above, this should not be done in blind obedience. We are all members of the body of Christ. For example, in Acts 15 the apostles and elders met together (verse 6) but then the whole church was involved in the final decision (verse 22). Not autocracy, but not democracy, but godly leadership that honours all, but also allows those with more prominent gifts to speak and give clarity to matters just as James (verse 7) and Peter (verse 13) did at that instructive gathering.

4. As appropriate, share the plunder, the victory you have shared in. Some of David's men who took more heat than others during the battle thought the others should not share fully in the victory. This was an ungodly attitude, contrasting that of David. So let us glorify God by sharing in the plunder he has given, some clear evidence of his having retrieved us, or someone else, back from abduction to sin or Satan. It might be being freed from bitterness, an illness; or some other form of divine deliverance.

QUESTIONS FOR REFLECTION OR DISCUSSION

1. What exactly do you now better appreciate about Jesus from this story?

2. Consider or share a time when you sensed God clearly spoke and told you to move *out* or *on* in obedience…and the result.

3. If you're an older mentor, share with your mentees a time when God clearly answered you after a desperate time of prayer, and what you did next.

4. Discuss a time when you or someone you know had a answer to prayer where God brought something or someone back. It may have involved:

   a. Binding an evil spirit in prayer or in ministering to someone afflicted in some way (as we saw in both Jesus and Paul's ministries already mentioned).

   b. Seeing someone set free from false teaching or deception by your persuading them, using as it were the 'sword of the Word' to slice through arguments against the knowledge of God, and retrieving the person captured by false teaching or someone who had taken them down a wrong path.[38]

   c. Was it rescuing someone from the darkness of sin and into the kingdom of light? i.e. God helping you see someone come to repentance and faith.

---

38. For example: *"Don't have anything to do with foolish and stupid arguments, because you know they produce quarrels. And the Lord's servant must not be quarrelsome but must be kind to everyone, able to teach, not resentful. Opponents must be gently instructed, in the hope that God will grant them repentance leading them to a knowledge of the truth, and that they will come to their senses and escape from the trap of the devil, who has taken them captive to do his will"* (2 Timothy 2:23-25 where Timothy is instructed how to gently handle someone opposing him / good teaching instead of being caught up with stupid and foolish arguments).

11

LOSS AND GRIEF

THE BACKGROUND

JUST WHEN YOU think it couldn't get any worse. David had just passed the biggest test so far of his leadership at Ziklag. God had enabled him to keep himself and his men together after their long march, the discovery of their burnt-out homes and absent families, potential mutiny, followed by a 24-hour battle to rescue everything and everyone. Now came more hard news. But this time David would not be able to retrieve someone he loved, and who had loved him; we looked at this relationship in an earlier chapter.

For David, a soul mate was gone.

> *After the death of Saul, David returned from striking down the Amalekites and stayed in Ziklag two days. On the third day a man arrived from Saul's camp with his clothes torn and dust on his head. When he came to David, he fell to the ground to pay him honor.*
>
> *"Where have you come from?" David asked him.*
>
> *He answered, "I have escaped from the Israelite camp."*
>
> *"What happened?" David asked. "Tell me."*

"The men fled from the battle," he replied. "Many of them fell and died. And Saul and his son Jonathan are dead."

Then David said to the young man who brought him the report, "How do you know that Saul and his son Jonathan are dead?"

"I happened to be on Mount Gilboa," the young man said, "and there was Saul, leaning on his spear, with the chariots and their drivers in hot pursuit. When he turned around and saw me, he called out to me, and I said, 'What can I do?'

"He asked me, 'Who are you?'

"'An Amalekite,' I answered.

"Then he said to me, 'Stand here by me and kill me! I'm in the throes of death, but I'm still alive.'

"So I stood beside him and killed him, because I knew that after he had fallen, he could not survive. And I took the crown that was on his head and the band on his arm and have brought them here to my lord."

Then David and all the men with him took hold of their clothes and tore them. They mourned and wept and fasted till evening for Saul and his son Jonathan, and for the army of the LORD and for the nation of Israel, because they had fallen by the sword.

David said to the young man who brought him the report, "Where are you from?"

"I am the son of a foreigner, an Amalekite," he answered.

David asked him, "Why weren't you afraid to lift your hand to destroy the LORD's anointed?"

Then David called one of his men and said, "Go, strike him down!" So he struck him down, and he died. For David had said to him, "Your blood be on your own head. Your own mouth testified against you when you said, 'I killed the LORD's anointed.'"

David took up this lament concerning Saul and his son Jonathan, and he ordered that the people of Judah be taught this lament of the bow – it is written in the Book of Jashar:

"A gazelle lies slain on your heights, Israel.
   How the mighty have fallen!

"Tell it not in Gath,
   proclaim it not in the streets of Ashkelon (two main cities)
lest the daughters of the Philistines be glad,
   lest the daughters of the uncircumcised rejoice.

"Mountains of Gilboa,
   may you have neither dew nor rain,
   may no showers fall on your terraced fields.
For there the shield of the mighty was despised,
   the shield of Saul—no longer rubbed with oil.

"From the blood of the slain,
   from the flesh of the mighty,
the bow of Jonathan did not turn back,
   the sword of Saul did not return unsatisfied.
Saul and Jonathan—
   in life they were loved and admired,
   and in death they were not parted.
They were swifter than eagles,
   they were stronger than lions.

"Daughters of Israel,
   weep for Saul,
who clothed you in scarlet and finery,
   who adorned your garments with ornaments of gold.

"How the mighty have fallen in battle!
   Jonathan lies slain on your heights.
I grieve for you, Jonathan my brother;
   you were very dear to me.
Your love for me was wonderful,
   more wonderful than that of women.

"How the mighty have fallen!
   The weapons of war have perished!"

2 Samuel 1 (insert and **bold** words mine)

THE END OF SAUL, AND DAVID'S REACTION

In Samuel's two-volume history (Books 1 and 2 of Samuel) we have reached halfway. David continues to rise, while Saul continues to decline. Saul's end arrives...in terrible fashion. Saul had proved himself an unworthy leader and his end was tragic, and devastating for the entire nation: battlefield suicide, the death of his sons, the end of his leadership. The Philistines ended up beheading him and pinning his body to a wall of his enemies' god. The writer of Chronicles offers an even clearer, additional perspective: Saul died *because he was unfaithful to the Lord...the Lord put him to death and turned the kingdom over to David* (1 Chronicles 10:13-14).

THE HEART OF THE TRUE KING

As with the opposition commander for whom David later wept and wrote a lament (see 2 Samuel 3) we see David's godly actions, his grief over the demise of the leaders of his country. No gloating. This is in keeping with our Lord Jesus. He mourns over even godless leaders, not rejoicing over the death of the wicked (Ezekiel 18:32).

Most leaders-in-waiting like David would be glad their arch enemy-on-the-inside was at last dead. Not David. In that sense he here better reflects the Messiah, Jesus. He is keenly aware that it was God who had entrusted Saul with the kingship, even if that trust was terribly abused and David had suffered under it. It was a time for mourning and not rejoicing. The country was void of any clear leadership, and their main enemy, the Philistines, had come right into the heart of the country, occupying many towns and villages the Israelites had abandoned in fear. The whole country was in a crisis – it was a national disaster. 'How the mighty have fallen' it says three times. The army had been whipped, a huge fall. Saul was stripped of his armour, the army of its weapons – 'The weapons of war had perished' (verse 31).

Here we pause to take a look at grief, consider its nature and how to best process it. This is what David was doing in using his God-given ability to write words and put them to song. David had lost a fellow soldier...and his best friend.

Losing a good friend

Not only was Jonathan a brave fighter and commander, frequently leading other soldiers in making inroads against the enemy, as the eldest son of King Saul he had also given up his right to the throne. He recognised that David would be the next king, not him. He yielded to what he saw as a divine plan, giving up a huge amount to help and encourage David, against his father's wishes. Yet he was ultimately loyal to his family and people and died fighting with them.

Apart from Samuel, who had been dead for years, no one was perhaps as clear about David's destiny as Jonathan had been. Thus no one appreciated Jonathan more than David. They covenanted together, promising steadfast love. Jonathan had made David promise that when he finally became king that he would remember Jonathan and his descendants (see chapter 14). He even contrasts Jonathan's devotion to that of his wives. He had lost a soul mate and was again thrown into distress. He was filled with grief and poured it out in the form of a poem that everyone was made to sing.

Finding a way

David found a way to express his grief. His poem was not only a way to remember those who had died but a way for everyone to express their grief. We see David's gratefulness and faith through it all. He clearly states, "I grieve for you, Jonathan my brother. You were very dear to me." We see how he personalised the statement. David was, as it were, standing by the graveside or memorial talking to him as if Jonathan was still there.

Yet mourning need not be over the death of a person we loved; it could be over the loss of a job, an important possession, a big opportunity, our health, or a circle of friends because we've moved location. It could be over a church or a business or a major project. Whatever the circumstances, it's crucial to work thoroughly through that loss – if you like, 'good grieving'. Failing to work through our grief only handicaps us. This is true of those in leadership as much as anyone else. Indeed, depending on our role, like David we may also need to help everyone *else* through the process and say some appropriate words as we deal with our own reaction to events.

RECOGNISING GRIEF AND ITS STAGES

In the 1960s, Granger Westberg, a professor on the faculty of both the medical and the divinity schools at Chicago University, USA, highlighted the clear connection between an individual's health and any unresolved grief. His short book, *Good Grief*, has sold millions of copies. He lists more grief stages than most experts in his field, but going through some of these stages is perfectly normal *and* completely necessary.

If you've suffered or are processing some loss or other then you will recognise or recall some of the stages. For you as a leader it is important in its own right; it's also important so that you recognise what your followers or a colleague at work may be going through. Your leadership will be more effective as a result and you will be known as someone with compassion who looks after his staff.

The stages Westberg identifies are these:

1. Shock.
2. Emotion poured out.
3. Depression and loneliness.
4. Distress.
5. Panic.
6. Guilt.
7. Anger and resentment.
8. Resisting returning to living as before but with the loss.
9. Gradual hope.
10. Affirming reality.

Even if grief is processed properly the stages are not experienced in some straight line; they can sometimes get blurred together and not all of them may be experienced.

Types of loss

Regardless of what or who we have lost, let me suggest four rough categories. They may of course overlap.

Some losses are *clean*. They may be very painful, but they are anticipated and less complicated, e.g. the death of an elderly relative who has been ill for some time, and to whom we've been able to say goodbye.

Some are *connected*. The loss raises issues in other areas. A young boy loses a grandfather he loved and knew well, but in the process it starkly exposes the absence of the other, living, grandfather who only ever had a faint interest in him. He's upset about the deceased grandparent, and now grieving about the absence of the living one who could, or should, have paid him more attention.

Some are *consuming*. This is when we lose someone or something especially close to our heart, or we suffer several losses around the same time, whether persons, possessions, or opportunities. I have a friend who lost a relative, a partner and then a good friend over a three-month period. It was a particularly hard time. We may not know which particular loss our heart is grieving over from one day to the next!

Some losses are *closed* – locked up. This is where we have simply been unable as yet, or unwilling, to recognise the loss. In time it comes out in other ways. I've a friend who lost his mother quite suddenly, but he didn't work through his grief thoroughly. Years later he suffered a panic attack at work for what seemed like no reason; he had no history of them. Why? After some counselling he slowly recognized that having just got engaged to his girlfriend it had triggered his unresolved grief over the sudden death of his mother years before. He finally acknowledged in full that she would not be sharing in the joy of the engagement, or the coming wedding. His mind finally registered his mother's permanent absence via the massive and concrete event of an engagement...and his body reacted. He had stayed at stage 1 or 2 (shock and then emotion poured out) for some time, and then many years later suddenly jumped to stage 5 (panic). It is of course a more dramatic demonstration of the kind of wave of emotion that can suddenly hit a grieving person. And it's not uniform. On the beach of grief you get some waves that are simply bigger than others, and they can take you by surprise at times, washing over your mind and heart.

Peace and quiet

Not only do we sometimes need the help of others, we sometimes need to be alone to process our grief. A hospital ward notice read, 'Quiet helps patients heal.' Here, what's true of the physical is true of the spiritual. There's a psalm in the Bible that is more well known than any other — Psalm 23. It is sometimes called 'The Shepherd's Psalm'. It says, "He leads me beside *quiet* waters. He refreshes my soul." Some people may find joining other believers in sung corporate worship difficult, even if they are extroverted; they may withdraw for a period of time from places where they will meet lots of people.

Expressing your grief and saying goodbye

Not everyone gets to say goodbye to a loved one who dies. David didn't. Some losses come suddenly, and in such cases the shock is just one initial stage of grief. You don't need to write it out like David did — he was used to writing things — but you do need to express your loss somehow. We explored this before in the chapter about isolation and depression (chapter 8). You might go for a walk or go somewhere that means a lot to you, meet with a friend, draw, paint, or sit quietly in some old church building. You might build a small but meaningful monument to that person or whatever it was you lost. That's why graves, memorial stones, benches with inscriptions, or flowers by the roadside in the case of a road traffic accident may help. Laying someone (or something) to rest is an important part of the process. Others may set up a charity in the memory of a loved one.

In terms of a memorial, I live quite near a beach, and I saw recently a memorial to a dog that clearly the owner had loved very much. And it was a small wooden box that the owner had fixed to a fence with some dog treats in it (for dogs passing with their owners). And on the box was written just some words of gratefulness about the friendship the dog had given him.

We don't know if David later went up Mount Gilboa where Jonathan died, but going to the place where we lost whatever it is we lost can, for some, be a part of the healing process. Whatever it is may be unique to you, and that's OK. Tributes and tears help make the grieving a healing process.

Another national tragedy

One man who suffered considerable trauma found an unusual route. In July 1987, an oil rig named *Piper Alpha* situated off the east coast of Scotland, my home country, exploded and resulted in the deaths of 167 people. Others had survived by leaping off the burning rig. One of them was Bill Barron, a painter. A memorial statue was commissioned by the city most affected by the tragedy. Bill drank heavily the year following the disaster. He did not find that group therapy helped. But one way he found he *could* talk more easily was with the artist, Sue Jane Taylor, who had been commissioned to build the memorial. Bill was asked to act as a life model. He stood perfectly still as the artist slowly crafted a large statue of oil men complete in their kit. He found he could talk more easily when he was standing there alone while Sue sculpted and talked with him. As I reflect on this, I see him as someone who had run and managed to escape the flames, but now later stood silently with those who could not escape. He identified with them, stood with them, in their death at work. It reminds me of Christ who chose to stand in our behalf, identifying with us. Jesus did this not by serving as a model for an important memorial, but by writhing in agony as he was nailed to a brutal cross.

PRACTICAL RELEVANCE

If we work through our grief properly, in due time we will be better able to help others struggling with grief. Some people don't know themselves, are not self-aware, don't realise the extent of their feelings. Many men tend to refrain from talking much and some end up emotionally incapacitated: they bottle it up. It's one reason why the suicide rate is much higher among men; we get buried in grief and depression and eventually can see only one way to escape, for good. It need not be this way, however.

I appeal to any men reading or listening to this: if you have successfully worked through significant loss, keep your eyes and ears open for men grieving over some type of loss. They may not know or fully appreciate what's going on inside of them, and how to deal with it, but they know they are screwed up inside. They may feel terrible some days, maybe every day, and want to end it all. Drugs, both legal and illegal, could be involved. You may know what this is like, so your presence alone may help them.

Church leaders and medical professionals are important here, but some people just need their friends extra close. Appreciate that like you, they have their own way and speed of grieving. And it's not a speed train. Most of the time we just need to shut up and simply be with people.

One grieving man who lost his wife to cancer was asked many years later what or who had meant the most to him immediately after her death. He replied, "A friend who came into the house after hearing the news sat down on the sofa, and wept." Sympathy, or empathy often need no words.

Whatever it is that you may be dealing with, may you find a way to process your grief or help someone else process theirs. In all, honour those God sends you, and grieve the good.

MAN OF SORROWS

> *He was despised and rejected by men,*
> *a man of sorrows and acquainted with grief.*
> Isaiah 53:3

Along with plenty of peace and quiet, what I've found helpful during times of loss has been meditating on Christ's sufferings on the cross, applying specific points to my own hurt. God is no stranger to suffering. Isaiah chapter 53 lists the different dimensions of his pain, including rejection and physical suffering. Christ suffered in innumerable ways and so can sympathise specifically with our pain. What's more, he undertook that suffering on a cross on our behalf to bring us back to God. Christ suffered much grief to bring you and I healing. We can now invite God into the grief process as we work through our losses. In him (Christ), God knows all about huge loss and pain; he knows us, and how we can best process our loss.

QUESTIONS FOR REFLECTION OR DISCUSSION

1. If you feel able, take Westwood's 10 stages, think to yourself, or with a friend, over a time of loss. Which of the stages did you experience? In which order did you experience them.

2. What *specifically* did you find helpful in processing your loss? What was *not* helpful?

3. Is there someone you need to stand with just now in their loss? If so, how specifically could you help them?

4. Consider meditating on Isaiah 53 and the Lord Jesus as the Man of Sorrows.

PART THREE:
KING

IN THIS SECTION we examine four more episodes in David's life. The first concerns David waiting on God for a long time, fighting before becoming king; the second about the covenant God made with David, and his response; the third about a time during the zenith of his reign where we see him at his most condescending, stooping to help someone in need; and the fourth and final chapter explores David's last words – a prayer – and how that relates to Christ the King.

Despite consistently obeying God in his first half before being crowned king, David actually ended up having a poor second half; the murder of Uriah and the taking of Bathsheba was the major blackspot which carried massive consequences and drastically affected his second half.[39] He had *despised* God, the same word used to describe Goliath's *contempt* for young David, a mere youth who had dared face him in battle (2 Samuel 17:42). Yet overall he did what was right, serving God's purpose in his generation (Acts 13:36).

I've not included a chapter covering that terrible episode, but I wrote a biblical monologue about it which is available online. It's called *The Abuse of Power and the Grace of God* and is a first-person message

---

39. 1 Kings 15:5 and the outworking of the sword that never departed from his own house as a result of his killing Uriah and taking Bathsheba (2 Samuel 12:10).

(first person POV)[40] based on 1 Samuel 10-12 and other background data. To accompany it, there is also a free 45-minute audiobook available on various platforms.

It is no guarantee of success, but leaders who pass through most of their first half tests by consistently nourishing themselves on the Lord will find themselves better placed for fruitful leadership over their lifetime since they will have learned valuable lessons, tending to always take things to the Lord – including, like David, when they fail. Ultimately, this was the difference between Saul and David. More often than not, David sought God for direction, whereas Saul often took matters into his own hands. One kept his anointing to lead and left a legacy; the other forfeited it.

---

40. For those interested, in literary terms it is classed as narrative non-fiction, not historical fiction. Preacher Haddon Robinson would occasionally preach in this way. I've done so a few times. There are newer books out there but one I've helpful is *Effective First-person Biblical Preaching* by J. Kent Edwards (2005).

CHAPTER

12

PATIENCE AND PROMOTION

"All my life is patience."[41]

Martin Luther, 16th Century
German theologian, preacher and reformer

"Patience is better than pride."

Ecclesiastes 7:8

Our reading is taken from 2 Samuel chapter 2 verses 1-7.

In the course of time, David inquired of the Lord. "Shall I go up to one of the towns of Judah?" he asked.

The Lord said, "Go up."

David asked, "Where shall I go?"

"To Hebron," the Lord answered.

So David went up there with his two wives, Ahinoam of Jezreel and Abigail, the widow of Nabal of Carmel. David also took the men who were with him, each with his family, and they settled in

---

41. Martin Luther in *Here I stand*, Roland Bainton (Lion Publishing, England: 1978) 301.

Hebron and its towns. Then the men of Judah came to Hebron, and there they anointed David king over the tribe of Judah.

*When David was told that it was the men from Jabesh Gilead who had buried Saul, he sent messengers to them to say to them, "The Lord bless you for showing this **kindness** to Saul your master by burying him. May the Lord now show you **kindness** and faithfulness, and I too will show you the same favor because you have done this. Now then, be strong and brave, for Saul your master is dead, and the people of Judah have anointed me king over them."*

2 Samuel 2:1-7 (emboldened words mine)

BACKGROUND AND DAVID'S RESPONSE

DAVID DID NOT seize power. He waited, he prayed, *then* he moved. He was later invited to take charge of the southern part of the country where he had come from, Judah, with Hebron being one of the main cities in that area. It served as David's first kingdom base and was situated about 20 miles south of Jerusalem.

First, David asked, "Shall I go up?" (the answer 'Go up'). "Where?" (the answer 'Hebron'). David got the counsel of someone higher up, in his case the Lord of heaven and earth. It's likely that he again sought the Lord and used the Urim and Thummim to cast lots. His context was one of a 'theocracy' in which the appointed king was God's vassal, an ancient Middle Eastern term for someone subject to another king's power and demands. For Israelite kings that counsel came not just through holy writings but through the advice of wise counsellors, the priest and messages from prophets.

Second, David also affirmed the men of Jabesh Gilead, a town further north and east, just across the Jordan River from where David was situated, and he tried to secure their loyalty. After Saul and his sons had died, the men of Jabesh Gilead had marched through the night to recover the bodies of King Saul and his three sons (one of whom of course was David's best friend, Jonathan). The reason for their loyalty in taking this risk was because decades earlier Saul had rescued them when an enemy had besieged their town. His heroic actions led to Samuel confirming Saul as king. It was Saul's leadership high point, showing that he was anointed as king to lead. Everybody had celebrated.[42] The men of Jabesh Gilead had not forgotten their history.

David twice uses the word 'chesed' (I'll just use the Anglicised 'hesed') which we have in English as kindness, and it means 'covenant loyalty'. It's a theme which occurs throughout David's life. It also applies to the Lord's loving kindness as well as human relationships. For example, we see it used also between David and Jonathan, and also David and Mephibosheth, which we'll see in a later chapter.

In a sense, the men of Jabesh Gilead had repaid Saul. Saul was no more, and David promised to support them as well. Hadn't he been anointed as the new king?

Since pro-Saul Jabesh Gilead is well north of Judah, it could have looked as if David was simply trying to smooth his way into taking over the whole country. There's an element of truth to that – David was not politically naïve. But his commending them was entirely consistent with how he had responded in all his dealings with Saul: he acted completely within character. And as we have seen before, his actions showed respect for Saul in his leadership position as king, even though Saul had tried several times to kill him.

In the seven years that follow before he was crowned king over all Israel, the narrator makes it clear that David was blameless in his actions. For example, when Joab his army commander unlawfully killed his opposite number, Abner, following a peaceful negotiation, David sang a lament over Abner in public (the same sort of thing he did as regards Jonathan and Saul when they died) and he arranged a public procession and burial for him, with David himself leading the way. The record stands:

> So on that day all the people there and all Israel knew that the king had no part in the murder of Abner son of Ner.
>
> **2 Samuel 3:37**

---

42. 1 Samuel 11

All this underlines that David was innocent...and patient. He did not take shortcuts.

GOD'S PROVISION AND HOW IT POINTS US TO CHRIST

David's coronation in Hebron and the support given him as the new King of Judah points us to Christ who in the last book of the Bible is named the 'Lion of Judah' (Revelation 5:5). As to his human nature, Jesus was descended from David. And as we have reflected on more than once, Jesus was also declared to be the Son of God in power by his resurrection from the dead (Romans 1:3-4). Jesus is the God-man who patiently waited to be crowned King of Kings, going through much suffering beforehand; like David, he obediently waited to be crowned.

On one occasion some of his followers tried to make him king by force. Having seen him miraculously feed thousands they concluded he was the one God had sent. They were right about that, but wrong about how he would go about things. It says in the Scriptures:

Jesus saw that they were ready to take him by force and make him their king, so he went higher into the mountains alone.

John 6:15

Many Jews at the time thought the Messiah would drive out the Romans and set up God's new kingdom in Israel. But his kingdom would not be geo-political. It was, and is not of this world but invades it and brings in God's rule; for example, healings, miracles, lives transformed by Christ. Jesus was aware of his Father's timing. His coronation would come later, after the suffering of the cross.

PRACTICAL RELEVANCE FOR LEADING

The importance of waiting

You may have gone to college or perhaps a university to gain an important qualification; that's fine and for many it's necessary. And yet gaining what you could call an M.C.A. (a Masters in *Character Acquisition*) as opposed to an M.B.A. (a Masters in *Business*

Administration) is far more important. The difference with God's *character* training courses is that for us the tuition is free, but it will cost a lot in other ways, and the syllabus is also unpredictable. You also don't know in advance when the exams are (apart from the last one) or even where they will be held. Fun, eh?

Many truly great leaders have found their route to greater influence sometimes blocked through various difficulties. This is no mistake. Waiting develops patience, an important character trait for any leader. And you don't develop patience by having everything going your way, or by forcing your own way. Or by lying on your résumé or your CV. Or by putting others in a bad light just so that you look better and get that promotion instead of them.

As David demonstrated, seeking God is crucial. And it can involve much waiting. It helps breed humility (waiting for your time) instead of sucking up to those in authority or who have connections (simply playing the game in order to get your way eventually).

A good biblical example of someone who had to wait for his time was the humble Old Testament leader, Moses. Being brought up in the Egyptian royal family he was "educated in all the wisdom of the Egyptians" and the other Scripture says he was "powerful in speech and action"(Acts 7:22). A more helpful start you could not imagine for someone in his day. Yet he later committed murder and fled the country. He then looked after sheep for 40 years in a desert far away before beginning an altogether different kind of leadership role in his second half. He then spent *another* 40 years leading his fellow people through a desert. In the Bible, the numeral 40 denotes 'testing'. He would never have been equipped for his main leadership task shepherding a whole nation through a desert in terms of his character had he not gone through his own lonely testing period in a desert. Any leader who has not been proven by testing will not lead people very far.

Waiting ensures perfect timing and clear backing

If you are meant to slot into a particular role, then waiting for others to invite you into it, into a clearly defined role, ensures a solid start and firm backing. People generally can't force their way into a leadership role, but they can smooth their way into position with conversations behind the scenes, or by making promises that once in power the person or group helping them will be rewarded or avoid being punished. Some involved or aware of how, for example, politicians tend to operate will think that waiting for ages is naive, but there's a difference between rewarding competence and support than sheer cronyism that ignores others who might do an equally good or a better job. Waiting for your time and refusing to worm your way into power lends great credibility to your start in a leadership role. It will be obvious to those who know you that you did not get into a position by sleight of hand, deceiving or colluding with some people in order to get your way.

I heard of one prospective elder who went around canvassing various families, asking for their vote to get him onto the eldership team. And of course that backfired, and he had to apologise to them all, and would have lost a great deal of credibility in the church.

It's better to be called into a role by God through others than by your own craftiness. Let David's testimony be yours. Let the Lord help you act patiently as you follow him in whatever sphere of service he has placed you. As someone once reminded me: Our Father in Heaven is the CEO of every company, organisation, and department. God is sovereign over the affairs of men, as King Nebuchadnezzar, one time leader of Babylon had to learn and acknowledge after going mad (insane) for a season:

> ...the Most High is sovereign over all kingdoms on earth and gives them to anyone he wishes.

Daniel 4:32

And psalm 75:

> No one from the east or the west or from the desert can exalt themselves. It is God who judges: he brings one down, he exalts another.

Psalm 75:6-7

"'The LORD declares to you that the LORD himself will establish a house for you: When your days are over and you rest with your ancestors, I will raise up your offspring to succeed you, your own flesh and blood, and I will establish his kingdom. He is the one who will build a house for my Name, and I will establish the throne of his kingdom forever. I will be his father, and he will be my son. When he does wrong, I will punish him with a rod wielded by men, with floggings inflicted by human hands. But my love will never be taken away from him, as I took it away from Saul, whom I removed from before you. Your house and your kingdom will endure forever before me; your throne will be established forever.'"

Nathan reported to David all the words of this entire revelation.

Then King David went in and sat before the LORD, and he said:

"Who am I, Sovereign LORD, and what is my family, that you have brought me this far? And as if this were not enough in your sight, Sovereign LORD, you have also spoken about the future of the house of your servant—and this decree, Sovereign LORD, is for a mere human!

"What more can David say to you? For you know your servant, Sovereign LORD. For the sake of your word and according to your will, you have done this great thing and made it known to your servant.

"How great you are, Sovereign LORD! There is no one like you, and there is no God but you, as we have heard with our own ears. And who is like your people Israel—the one nation on earth that God went out to redeem as a people for himself, and to make a name for himself, and to perform great and awesome wonders by driving out nations and their gods from before your people, whom you redeemed from Egypt? You have established your people Israel as your very own forever, and you, LORD, have become their God.

> *"And now, Lord God, keep forever the promise you have made concerning your servant and his house. Do as you promised, so that your name will be great forever. Then people will say, 'The Lord Almighty is God over Israel!' And the house of your servant David will be established in your sight.*
>
> *"Lord Almighty, God of Israel, you have revealed this to your servant, saying, 'I will build a house for you.' So your servant has found courage to pray this prayer to you. Sovereign Lord, you are God! Your covenant is trustworthy, and you have promised these good things to your servant. Now be pleased to bless the house of your servant, that it may continue forever in your sight; for you, Sovereign Lord, have spoken, and with your blessing the house of your servant will be blessed forever."*

KNIVES AND FORKS, PICKS AND PLECTRUMS

Nathan received a 'revelation' which he then *reported to David*. David received this as a prophecy, a prophetic word. Nathan didn't receive a 'teaching', and David didn't receive a 'teaching'.

I'd like to first distinguish between the understanding we are given as we study the words of Scripture and apply it to our lives (or hear some teaching), compared to something God may reveal to us in some other way, e.g. through a dream, vision, or some other clear sense of God speaking to us directly apart from when studying the Scriptures, just as we see with Nathan.

The first, studying the Bible, involves *applying the mind*, asking the Holy Spirit to 'illuminate', to give us understanding of the Word of God as we seek to interpret it responsibly. It's like God is shining a flashlight / torch when we are reading. This should involve at the very least getting the sentence or passage we're studying in context. Context is king. A helpful book I mentioned before is *Journey into God's Word* by Duvall and Hays (2nd edition, 2020). I've taken groups of younger men through it over a 15-week period. It's essentially an abbreviated version of a first-year Bible college interpretation class which helps the reader learn five steps in understanding and applying Scripture. It's like using a knife and fork, cutting up and learning to digest what's before us, and it's necessary for going from milk to solid food. And it must be central to discipling others, so that they learn how to feed themselves and grow in maturity so they can learn to take on responsibility for others (Hebrews 5:11 – 6:3).

Second, receiving a *revelation* like Nathan did involves *receiving something in our spirit*. It's more like using a plectrum or a pick used to play a guitar *as a song comes to us*. I'm no musician, but some musicians say that a song 'just came to them'. It's something they received, something 'given'. It's the same with receiving a *revelation*. It's a matter of receiving images or words that are given to us. And it's why a *revelation* (which when spoken becomes prophecy), is something given to a person's spirit and can sometimes be connected to or inspired by music.

The prophet Elisha once asked for a harpist to help him hear from the Lord – he knew it might help (2 Kings 3:15). It's also why Christ gives teachers *and* prophets among us (see Acts 13:1-3). Silas, who accompanied Paul and Timothy and helped them pen some letters to the churches, was not a Bible teacher; like Judas, he exercised a prophetic ministry, saying much to encourage and strengthen believers (Acts 15:32; 1 Corinthians 14:3).[43] It was the same in the Old Testament. For example, in Ezra we see Ezra himself, a teacher; but also Haggai and Zechariah, both prophets (Ezra 5:1-2; 7:8-10). In Old Testament times the words of the prophets held more sway as they were 'the word of the Lord'. Rebel against a true prophet and his word, or her words,[44] and you were rebelling against God. Not so today, because we prophesy in part: we don't understand everything (1 Corinthians 13:9-13).

In some Christian circles there's a danger of getting *teaching* and *revelation* mixed up. We use our *mental skills* and pray for the Spirit's illumination as we study Scripture, for Jesus to open up the Scriptures

---

43. 1 and 2 Thessalonians was written by Paul *and* Silas *and* Timothy. He wrote 6 of his letters alone; the rest were team affairs, just like the rest of his apostolic ministry. Paul was no 'lone ranger' or an autocratic leader who ordered people around.
44. For example, Miriam (Exodus 15), Deborah (Judges 4), Huldah (2 Kings 22), Noadiah [false] (Nehemiah 6), Isaiah's wife (Isaiah 8), and Anna (Luke 2).

to us. (Those who regularly teach the Bible may also find themselves making wee sermon notes as they read, thinking how this or that section or chapter could be crafted into a sermon.) It can sometimes be hard work, but joyful work, like cutting up a tough piece of meat with a knife and fork, but then we taste the meat, we experience the joy of discovery. But what we don't do is wait for some moment of *revelation* that then ignores the basic rules of grammar and context any more than we might sit there with a steak in front of us and expect it to somehow climb into our mouth by itself. God grants understanding *as we pray and search the Scriptures,* comparing Scripture with Scripture as well as getting a sense of the broader story of the Bible.

The idea of waiting to 'get *a revelation*' as we sit with the Bible (regardless of the context of the verse or the passage) can be tied back to the idea of a 'logos' word versus a 'rhema' word. This is discussed more fully in Appendix A at the end of this book. Sadly, this approach to understanding or teaching the Bible results in a lack of maturity: people don't learn to pick up their knife and fork. And it's also where false teachings can come in. For example, pastor X says he's had a revelation about some passage in the Bible. It sounds credible and exciting, especially to those less used to picking up their knife and fork and applying their minds and examining the Scriptures (see Acts 17:11). But if it's taken out of context, it's not from God. It doesn't matter how it makes us feel. God can and does take individual verses and sheds light on them for us, or uses them to speak directly to us in a special way, just not out of context.

For example, a friend of mine said that he woke up in the middle of night with Deuteronomy 2:2 in his mind. He had no idea what it said so he went and looked it up. He began reading, "Then the LORD said to me: 'You have made your way around this hill country long enough; now turn north.'" In his context, for years he had been traveling 150 miles south every week with his job. He had been wondering if he should call it a day, hand in his resignation. That experience and specific verse clinched it. God the Spirit had prompted him to open his Bible at a specific verse. To the original hearers it also literally meant 'turn north'. So we're on solid ground.

Most believers will have experienced this sort of thing in regularly reading their Bible and seeking God for guidance. Just not 'lucky dip' where we open the Bible at random in the hope that some verse or other will stick out to us, but reading through the Bible, trusting God to speak by highlighting something specific to us when we need it, as well as learning and applying biblical principles as we unearth them in our study of Scripture. Reading and studying and meditating and memorising – all excellent and vital ways to get the word of God into our system.

As to the other matter, a *revelation*, we don't use a knife and fork (our intellectual skills) to *receive* a *revelation, or to interpret it.* But we *do* consult our Bible about the *principles* of interpretation, whether regarding dreams or visions or other ways God speaks directly to people. For example, when Joseph listened to the cupbearer and baker of the king of Egypt, he stated, "Do not interpretations belong to God? Tell me your dreams." (Genesis 40:8). Two years later, when Pharoah king of Egypt summoned him regarding interpreting the king's own dreams, Joseph replied, "I cannot do it, but God will give Pharoah the answer he desires" (Genesis 41:16).

Interpretation of dreams (and tongues for that matter) belongs to God. It's not in us, it's not something that we can intellectually work out. It's not about having a brilliant mind or a strong intellect (a big asset for any Bible teacher.) Just as we don't sit down and apply our God-given mental skills to *receive* a dream or other kind of revelation (such as a vision or even a trance – Acts 10:10), we shouldn't seek to *interpret* such things using primarily our cognitive skills. We don't disconnect our minds, but we can meditate or treasure up what God has revealed to us, just like Mary did (Luke 2:19). Or if it is not immediately clear, seek God for the interpretation. In that sense dreams are not self-interpreting. Some of it may concern the future, so we may not fully understand things until they come to pass; nor may we sense permission to share the dream with anyone.

In the case of Joseph in Matthew's account of the good news (Matthew 1 and 2), an angel speaks to him very clearly in a dream about what he needed to do – a powerful dream, with very clear instructions.

It was the same with the vision of an angel given to Zechariah, and the angelic visitations Mary and the shepherds experienced (Luke 1 and 2).

In Acts chapter 8 we read that God spoke to Philip via an angel, telling him to go to a desert road. The Spirit then spoke directly to Philip, telling him to stay close to a chariot. We then read of Philip *explaining* to an important government official from the region of Ethiopia the good news *from the Scriptures*. So in this one story we see both *revelation* and *teaching*, the second of which involves understanding Scripture and it's message. Two different things.

Daniel went on a partial fast as he prayed for the understanding about a message he had received; the explanation of the message was given to him through a vision (Daniel 10:1-2). Of interest for us on this topic is that he also *'understood from the Scriptures'* on a separate occasion (Daniel 9:2). In both situations it involved much prayer. But in one he understood from the Scriptures, in the other through a vision: two different ways God communicated with him.

These two examples from Daniel's life and Philip's life illustrate the difference between a *teaching* (or interpretation of Scripture) and a *revelation*. Both involve being given understanding, of God revealing things to us, but they are two different categories of how God can and does speak to people by his same Holy Spirit.

I once received a dream, the meaning of which was simply not clear. So I boldly asked for another dream to interpret the first, and God graciously granted my request. While not everything was clear, the overall picture was clearer than before. God gave me a revelation in the form of dream one, and then gave me some understanding of dream one via another revelation, dream two. God is gracious, and will give us understanding as we submit to and ask him.

Sometimes receiving a revelation needs no action other than being willing to listen; for example, someone shares with us what turns out to be an accurate and encouraging prophecy; or we are fast asleep one night and God clearly speaks to us in the form of a dream. Or perhaps when we're waiting on God in prayer he reveals something to us that we are later given permission from him to share. A *teaching* or a *revelation* from God both involve the role of the Holy Spirit.

Though one of my main gifts is teaching, I can testify to having received revelations and given prophecies (a revelation that is shared somehow). Prophetic words can come to us when we're praying on our own, with others, for someone else, or for a group of people, or over a particular matter. As to dreams, for me it has involved asking the Lord over a series of nights before getting into bed, asking him to speak in this way. While it doesn't say that Joseph asked for dreams, he received four, all concerning the Saviour (Matthew 1 and 2). Encouraged by this, I've been able to testify to my many Muslim friends that God has spoken to me very clearly in this way (and pray the same for them). If there's genuine friendship that has been established over time, it's not so easy to dismiss. For those who follow the teachings of Islam, personal dreams are one of the few ways Allah might speak to you personally.

God is the God of dreams as much as he is the God of the Bible, and the Scripture teaches us how to handle dreams. God may test our willingness and faith in this: if we pray just once and then give up, it might show that we don't really believe or desire for God to speak to us in this way. If we apply that to studying the Bible, would we give up after just one attempt in trying to interpret a passage?

To conclude this section, just as some in more charismatic circles can lose their biblical moorings in seeking the miraculous, so too can some more conservative believers or churches limit the Spirit's work largely to studying the Bible, Bible teaching, circumstances, and a few other ways God guides, but not really the miraculous. Yet this can rob us of the richness of the other ways God can speak to us in addition to the centrality of reading and hearing the Scriptures; for example, dreams, visions, and other types of revelation, which ironically the Bible itself teaches about, as we've seen. As Paul urged: 'Follow the way of love and eagerly desire gifts of the Spirit, especially the gift of prophecy' (1 Corinthians 14:1). Not either/or, the Bible (or teaching) and revelation, but *both*. For more on this in terms of teaching and revelation please read appendix B at the end of the book (More or less of the Spirit?)

A HEALTHY RESPONSE, CHRIST, AND SOME PRACTICALITIES

In this chapter I will intertwine the aspects of context, Christ, and some applications for today.

1. *Humility.* David sat down before the Lord, overwhelmed. 'Is this your usual way of dealing with people?' David asked. 'Who am I?' 'What is my family?' All this is evidence that he was awestruck as to how the Almighty had spoken to him. It was the same with Moses, and Gideon. It's a healthy response: no flippancy as to how the Lord had spoken to him. That sense of awe can occur because of how daunting the leadership task ahead is (as in the case of Moses and Gideon). But here David is being promised something, not being commanded to do something.

If you or I are overcome by something we sense that God has spoken to us then it's a good response. Youthfulness may lead some to blurt out naively what God may have in fact spoken; for example, where young Joseph spoke to his father and brothers about their bowing before him, much to their annoyance (Genesis 37), but it is usually better to keep it to ourselves. God confides in those who fear him (Psalm 25:14), not in those who gossip or who have not learned discretion.

As suggested elsewhere, writing things down somewhere in private afterwards is wise advice (for dreams, doing this immediately is best). Sometimes the matter can be in public to begin with; for example, young David being anointed by Samuel in front of his whole family and the town elders (1 Samuel 16:4-13). After the dust settles, we may see some initial fulfilment (in David's case, with the anointing he began vigorously defending the sheep from lions and bears by the power of the Spirit). But more often than not we don't see much fulfilment at the beginning.

Revelation often involves waiting. Patience will need to be developed. But here we're talking about an immediate and appropriate posture when we sense God has clearly spoken to us about something, perhaps like David about our future. In many cases, wonder will be a natural reaction. Let's keep it that way. Revisiting the sense of amazement and thanking God for speaking to us in the way he did will help us if we are tempted to get ahead of ourselves and make friends with Mr. Impatience, or Mrs. Forgetful.

Had David stopped more often to consider all that God had done for him, including the entire revelation Nathan reported to him, then he might not have so easily called for Bathsheba that fateful day on the rooftop when he happened to see her bathing (2 Samuel 11). It might have led him again to stop and give thanks to God, and in return for all that God had done for him to better use his time, continue to exercise leadership, and not become lazy and send Joab out instead to go to battle in his place.[45]

2. *David responded to the Lord as God.* It is entirely consistent with the awe of the occasion – solemnity. David here uses the phrase *Sovereign LORD* (NIV) seven times. It's the *only* time it occurs in the whole of 1 and 2 Samuel. Seven times, on David's lips. It's a combination of two names for God [*Yahweh* or YHWH, the divine name; and *Adonai* meaning Lord). Both were also used together by Abraham when God made a covenant with him (Genesis 15:2 and 8; Deuteronomy 9:26). They were also used by Moses when he fasted for 40 days and nights, pleading with the *Sovereign LORD* for the people of Israel after they had sinned by creating and attributing to a calf made of gold their miraculous deliverance from Egypt.

David also used twice what we have in the English NIV as *LORD Almighty.* It means the 'Lord of Hosts' (elsewhere many times 'army' or 'armies'). Interestingly, David also used it when addressing Goliath: 'I come against you in the name of the *LORD Almighty*' (1 Samuel 17:45). As then, David was conscious of the Lord of the hosts [powers] in heaven and earth. He knew he wasn't alone.

---

45. In 2 Samuel 10 we see the seeds of David's fall as he first *sends* out Joab when he should have been leading, then later *sends* for Bathsheba, then *sends* for Uriah before God *sent* Nathan. In breaking all those commandments David abused his power in sending…and taking.

Have you ever had such an experience of God that you found it hard to find the right words, perhaps some name for God, a holy name? I heard one man just entering a new leadership role state publicly that if he had known the Hebrew for 'Amazing God' he would have used the phrase. He was just *so* thankful to God for the way he had opened up the way for him to get there. He didn't provide all the details, but his sense of gratefulness was obvious.

Or perhaps like Paul you do not sense divine permission to share too much, maybe nothing at all; it was just too holy a moment. Paul wrote:

> *And I know that this man—whether in the body or apart from the body I do not know, but God knows — was caught up to paradise and heard inexpressible things, things that no one is permitted to tell.*

2 Corinthians 12:3-4

Sometimes this is solid advice, particularly if we sense God has promised us something, that he will do something in our lifetime, or even after (like the prophet Daniel, and much less common). It's also a safety net: we can end up looking like a false prophet if we predict or declare things that don't end up happening. In David's case there was an initial fulfilment in terms of his son, Solomon, succeeding him. Remarkable when we think about it: Solomon entered the world as the result of an adulterous affair, after the murder of his mother's first husband, one of David's best fighting men. Solomon's older sibling also died within a week of birth (2 Samuel 11-12).

3. *David gave God glory in his response* by stating how great God is, but also recounting his dealings with his people. 'How great you are!' David exclaimed. He then went on to say how unique God is, and his saving acts to redeem and bless a people (Israel) and establish them as his people (verses 22-24).

We can take each of these phrases and carry them right into the New Testament and be edified. Unless you are a believing Jew, God

Ziba answered the king, "There is still a son of Jonathan; he is lame in both feet."

"Where is he?" the king asked.

Ziba answered, "He is at the house of Makir son of Ammiel in Lo Debar."

So King David had him brought from Lo Debar, from the house of Makir son of Ammiel.

When Mephibosheth son of Jonathan, the son of Saul, came to David, he bowed down to pay him honor.

David said, "Mephibosheth!"

"At your service," he replied.

"Don't be afraid," David said to him, "for I will surely show you kindness for the sake of your father Jonathan. I will restore to you all the land that belonged to your grandfather Saul, and you will always eat at my table."

Mephibosheth bowed down and said, "What is your servant, that you should notice a dead dog like me?"

Then the king summoned Ziba, Saul's steward, and said to him, "I have given your master's grandson everything that belonged to Saul and his family. You and your sons and your servants are to farm the land for him and bring in the crops, so that your master's grandson may be provided for. And Mephibosheth, grandson of your master, will always eat at my table." (Now Ziba had fifteen sons and twenty servants.)

Then Ziba said to the king, "Your servant will do whatever my lord the king commands his servant to do." So Mephibosheth ate at David's table like one of the king's sons.

Mephibosheth had a young son named Mika, and all the members of Ziba's household were servants of Mephibosheth. And Mephibosheth lived in Jerusalem, because he always ate at the king's table; he was lame in both feet.

2 Samuel chapter 9

WHY DID DAVID RESPOND THE WAY HE DID?

The text does not tell us why Jonathan's name popped into David's head. Maybe it was someone he saw that day that reminded him of his military peer from all those years ago. Maybe it was something he read. Whatever prompted him to think back, we see David at his best as a man of compassion, not just a soldier and leader.

Memories and promises

As we know, Jonathan was David's contemporary and rightful heir to the throne. But he had recognised in David God's chosen man for the task of leading the country, and sacrificed much to help him. Here was a man, put in contemporary terms, who would take a bullet for David, and more than once.

In a touching scene several decades before, probably when both of them were in their early 20s, Jonathan had helped David escape the clutches of his deranged father, and the two of them said goodbye for what they knew could be the last time. Forged in many battles and possessing a similar outlook, their bond ran very deep. Knowing that they might not see each other ever again, they made sworn promises of friendship. Jonathan urged David not to forget him.

> *"May the LORD be with you as he has been with my father (King Saul). But show me unfailing kindness like the LORD's **kindness** as long as I live, so that I may not be killed, and do not ever cut off your **kindness** from my family". So Jonathan made a covenant with the house of David, saying, "May the LORD call David's enemies to account." And Jonathan had David reaffirm his oath out of love for him, because he loved him as he loved himself.*
>
> **1 Samuel 20:14-17** *(**bold** words mine)*
>
> *David...bowed down before Jonathan three times, with his face to the ground. Then they kissed each other and wept together—but David wept the most. Jonathan said to David, "Go in peace, for we have sworn friendship with each other in the name of the Lord,*

saying 'The LORD is witness between you and me, and between your descendants and my descendants forever.'" Then David left, and Jonathan went back to the town.

1 Samuel 20:41-42

The same man who had years before removed Goliath's massive head and carried it into the capital city was humbly reduced to a watery mess. In their culture at that time, as is still the case in the Middle East and other regions of the world today, men are more tactile with each other than those in the West. Many Western men only get physical with each other when someone dies, or during sport when someone scores a point or a goal.

David realised full well the extent of the love shown to him. He did not fail to remember their deep friendship, their sworn promises to each other, and Jonathan's incredible kindness in giving up so much for David. But Jonathan had died many years before and couldn't 'cash in his chips' as it were and ask a favour from David: "Keep your promise and show kindness to any descendants I have left".

The word *kindness* appears several times in English and twice in the original, and is a word David often used. Bible translations use it, e.g. at the end of Psalm 23, translating it as God's *loving kindness* or *steadfast love*. It's that Hebrew word again 'chesed' (English – *hesed*). It can be kindness expressed by God for people, or between people.

Jonathan's son Mephibosheth

From a single sentence inserted in an earlier chapter we learn that on a single day at the tender age of 5 Mephibosheth had suffered immensely. Not only did he lose his father and grandfather, he lost the use of both of his feet. On hearing the news of Jonathan and Saul's death in battle, Mephibosheth's nurse grabbed him and fled for safety. He probably broke both his ankles when he fell trying to escape. Perhaps she fell on top of him; but whatever, you couldn't reset them in those days.

We read about it in 2 Samuel 4:4.

> *Jonathan son of Saul had a son who was lame in both feet. He was five years old when the news about Saul and Jonathan came from Jezreel. His nurse picked him up and fled, but as she hurried to leave, he fell and became disabled. His name was Mephibosheth.*

Not only that, Mephibosheth lost his inheritance in the ensuing civil war as his family's power declined. Indeed, as his family's influence declined as part of God's judgment his very life was at risk, whether he was able-bodied or not. New kings would typically deal strongly with those connected with the previous king.

HOW THE STORY POINTS TO JESUS

Greatness and lameness

If you want an image of a powerful yet caring and personal God then this is a tremendous story. David here exemplifies a king who is powerful, who keeps his promises, welcomes us to his table to eat with his family, and gently embraces us in all our weaknesses – every day. It's demonstrated in the cross of Christ and the night before when Jesus and his disciples gathered around a table. Jesus broke bread and got them to share a cup of wine, giving them a clear image of his body and blood, about to be broken and spilled the very next day. He gathered them around a table. Like a lamb being slaughtered he was to offer himself up as an innocent sacrifice. This should be seen in contrast to his bravery and greatness. God became a man and humbled himself, even to death on a cross (Philippians 2:5).

For those willing to see it, the cross is *the* greatest act of bravery, humility and sacrifice. Churches today call it communion, or the Lord's Supper, recalling that dramatic event when Christ laid down his life for the sins of the world.

Someone else who is lame

Like Mephibosheth we are lame, but in heart, rather than in feet. We too have fallen, not from running away, but from God's righteous standards. People crippled by what the Bible calls sin: rebellion against

QUESTIONS FOR REFLECTION OR DISCUSSION

1. How would you have felt if you were Mephibosheth?

2. What's your personal experience as regards being aware of your own sinful brokenness and experiencing Christ's loving kindness in calling and forgiving you, and feeding you every day?

3. Like David, have you made a promise to someone you now need to fulfil?

4. How can hospitality show itself in your leadership or the leadership of those you look up to? How could you foster it in your team or your department, your home, your life?

5. If it's in your power to help, is there someone who needs something restored to them?

6. Is there someone needy, or a needy group of people you or your family or organisation could help?

7. Mephibosheth was a complete nobody. Do you get embarrassed associating with people who stand out, those on the margins? How could you change that?

CHAPTER

15

DAVID'S LAST WORDS

TAKING THE SAME approach as in the rest of this book, after first considering what it would have meant in its original setting, we will take it right into the New Testament and see its greater fulfilment in Christ. While more difficult to communicate in writing, my hope and my prayers long before writing this are that this last chapter will honour God, and give those who will read it, or listen to it on audiobook, a due sense of awe as we consider the magnificence of Christ, and how God wonderfully fulfilled his promise, and will one day consummate that same kingdom.

Psalm 72 – David's last words.

Endow the king with your justice, O God,
  the royal son with your righteousness.
May he judge your people in righteousness,
  your afflicted ones with justice.

May the mountains bring prosperity to the people,
  the hills the fruit of righteousness.
May he defend the afflicted among the people
  and save the children of the needy;
  may he crush the oppressor.
May he endure as long as the sun,
  as long as the moon, through all generations.

May he be like rain falling on a mown field,
like showers watering the earth.
In his days may the righteous flourish
and prosperity abound till the moon is no more.

May he rule from sea to sea
and from the River to the ends of the earth.
May the desert tribes bow before him
and his enemies lick the dust.
May the kings of Tarshish and of distant shores
bring tribute to him.
May the kings of Sheba and Seba
present him gifts.
May all kings bow down to him
and all nations serve him.

For he will deliver the needy who cry out,
the afflicted who have no one to help.
He will take pity on the weak and the needy
and save the needy from death.
He will rescue them from oppression and violence,
for precious is their blood in his sight.

Long may he live!
May gold from Sheba be given him.
May people ever pray for him
and bless him all day long.
May grain abound throughout the land;
on the tops of the hills may it sway.
May the crops flourish like Lebanon
and thrive like the grass of the field.
May his name endure forever;
may it continue as long as the sun.

Then all nations will be blessed through him,
and they will call him blessed.

Praise be to the LORD *God, the God of Israel,*
  who alone does marvelous deeds.
Praise be to his glorious name forever;
  may the whole earth be filled with his glory.
Amen and Amen.

This concludes the prayers of David son of Jesse.

Psalm 72

BACKGROUND

David understood that his kingdom would last forever, and here we explore his last words, essentially a prayer for his son, King Solomon.

At the end of 1 Chronicles we see him gathering all the officials, leaders and fighting men in his kingdom. He addressed the people gathered, and charged Solomon to obey God and follow his commands: serve him with your whole heart. Central to the handover was the temple that David wanted to build but was not permitted to do so. So he had made extensive preparations and publicly handed Solomon the plans God had given him before praising God and praying for Solomon. And after declaring all that he had provided out of his personal resources for the temple he asked those present to do the same. The temple was for God, not man. By the end everybody there was flat on their face in worship, in honour of God and the king. The next day they sacrificed thousands of cattle and anointed Solomon as king. It was a time of great awe one day and fantastic celebration the next.

Politically it was important to ensure a smooth transition of power and the stability of the kingdom. And far more importantly was the spiritual and religious significance. God had promised David that through his son, Solomon, he would build an everlasting kingdom. The temple was a physical sign of this.

This prayer for Solomon expresses David's desires for the type, length and scope of Solomon's reign. David pieces together under divine inspiration words that also point to another type of king and the length and scope and impact of *his* reign. David has, if you like, prophetically one eye on Solomon, and another on the Sovereign who is God, the one who not only blessed the installing of Solomon as king, but the one would one day install his own Son as king.[48]

THE TYPE OF LEADER WE ALL NEED

Since the psalms are best communicated as words and images that we sense, feel, and experience more than just understand mentally and put into categories, for this chapter I've merged the chapter goals together, moving more fluidly from what the psalm would have meant then, to how it applies and can be felt today, especially as to how it relates to Christ. We'll reflect on some of the images.

The people then needed a good king whose leadership would save them from their enemies. A king whose righteous rule would mean blessing and salvation for them. A king who would rule in righteousness and justice (v 1-4), rescuing those under oppression (v 12-14). A king whose reign would not shrink over the years but last forever (v 5-7), guaranteeing eternal security for all those under his rule. A king whose reign would reach even us, to the ends of the earth! (v 8-11). One who would therefore be blessed by the people and in him all nations would be blessed (v 15-19).

As we can legitimately do with Old Testament figures opposed to the people of God, we can take them as representing things from which we today need delivered. We saw this with Goliath, a giant enemy of Israel. It shows us that we are poor and needy and need to be delivered from oppression and death. We need a great king to save us.

Kingship then and now

Psalm 72 says a lot about the nature of the kingdom we actually need, and the type of king we need in charge. As with all other nations at that time and in that region, the Israelites would have understood that they had a complete ruler at the helm – the lawgiver. From Deuteronomy 17 they would also have appreciated that the king was

---

48. Psalm 2

God's vassal, God's appointed leader who was to obey God and not think of himself as being above everyone else.

If you're reading or listening to this and you are from the West or a westernised country, you made need reminded that if you are a follower of Christ, you are not an independent individual in some heavenly democracy. Believers are subjects of the King no matter where they live; living here on earth, yet citizens of Heaven (Philippians 3:20). Those who live in countries where there is a king with power, will better relate to this idea. But we will all recall the second line of the Lord's prayer: 'Our Father who is in heaven, your kingdom come.' God is king!

THE TYPE AND EFFECT OF HIS REIGN (v1-4 and 12-14)

Crushed (v 4)

Literally...smashed to pieces. If you've ever stood on an insect / bug you'll recall the squished mess underneath. It's not going to gather itself together again to mount an attack against you. This was David's wish for Solomon's enemies, that they would be crushed, smashed to pieces.

David had seen many of his enemies crushed. Again and again God had given him the victory. God had also *delivered* (v 12) David from the lion and bear, and he delivered him from Goliath (1 Samuel 17:37). It's the same word in the original. We saw in a previous chapter David *delivering*, i.e. *rescuing* everyone, *recovering* everything. Again, it's the same word. Not only will this king crush the enemy, he will deliver the needy. Both are needed: crushing and delivering. Through his death and resurrection Jesus crushed Satan and delivered us from the grip of sin and death. And his plan is to free people from every nation.

Have you been set free? Are you experiencing that freedom today or are you being weighed down by some sin or other hindrance? Let's look to our deliverer and king who has crushed the enemy and will completely and finally end his work upon his return. Let's work with him in seeing people set free from sin, and from patterns of sinful behaviour (this is where discipleship is so key: discipling people so that they become in practice what they are already in position by virtue of the cross and resurrection).[49]

Rain (v 6)

I like to play golf. If you play last thing at night or early in the morning the dew settles on the tightly mown grass. It's quite a sight, like a giant spider's web being stretched across hundreds of yards of finely cut grass, catching the occasional glint of fading or growing sunlight; life-giving water like rain, settling on grass and flowers alike. In desert areas dew in the later or early hours is crucial to plant life as well as insects and animals. Rain and dew – these are like the effect of a righteous king's leadership: life-giving. Let's give thanks for the Lord's amazing life-giving leadership, his rule that sustains our lives.

THE SCOPE AND EFFECT OF HIS REIGN

Dust (v 9)

Have you ever seen someone get faceplanted into the ground when they fall? Maybe it's happened to you. It's happened to me! Hopefully on the beach or something and not a hard surface. Having sand or gravel in your mouth as a result is no fun. Feel the grains of sand, of dirt, swirling around in your mouth: a grotesque mouthwash.

The king's enemies were to *lick the dust*. Made to submit. Crawl on their bellies like a snake. Humiliated. For those in the Middle East and some Asian countries the image is more potent than for those in the West where people don't tend to take off their shoes before they enter a house. Dragging dirt and dust from outside is incredibly rude. How much more making someone *lick* what's been on the sole of your feet. This is what the king was to do as part of the extent of his reign in reaching even desert places and places where dust is more prominent. This is what King David hoped for Solomon his successor. And it's the hope of the kingdom, the effect of Christ's death on the cross. For

---

49. A key message of Romans 6 – 8.

there in the humiliation of the cross Jesus made a public spectacle of his enemies (Colossians 2:15).

Gold (v 10 and 15)

That most pliable and glamorous of metals. As with other parts of David's prayer this was soon fulfilled, initially. He had provided lots of gold himself, and the others there followed suit, just as they had in Moses' time for the Tabernacle (Exodus 35). It was used to line the inside of parts of the temple and the items in it. People bringing their gifts, surrendering their possessions, and paying homage to the king, and God. People from the South (Sheba – see 1 Kings 10 and the Queen of Sheba) as well as the West (Tarshish, i.e. Spain). The Queen of Sheba provided around 4 tons of gold. Well, what does that look like?

Well, in 2011 the Australian Mint produced a one-ton gold coin.[50] It's the biggest and most expensive coin in the world: 31 inches (80 cm) in diameter and 4.5 inches (12 cm) wide; a bit like a thin car wheel. The Queen of Sheba presented to Solomon the equivalent of *four* of these!

It speaks to us now of individuals surrendering their possessions in homage to the King of the Ages, of people paying homage to the King of Heaven, of people giving back to Christ the King what is his, giving their time and talents to see the kingdom of God extended, the King's rule expanded. And if we think that gold is worth hoarding for ourselves here, let's not forget that in heaven it's used to line the streets like tar (Revelation 21:21). And we can't take it with us from here.

Last...

BLESSED BE HIS NAME! (v 15-19)

Like some crescendo of a magnificent anthem, David's words rise at the end to shout out praise to a king whose reign impacts all nations, that *all* might call him blessed because he has blessed them, that the

---

50. https://www.globalintergold.info/en/how-does-a-ton-of-gold-look-like-zo137/ Accessed June 2021

whole earth would be filled with his glory (Habakkuk 2:14). As Moses wrote and Isaiah saw, the whole earth *is* filled with his glory (Numbers 14:21 and Isaiah 6), but there is coming a day – the consummation of the kingdom – when the whole earth will be filled, entirely submitted to Christ the King (1 Corinthians 14:24-28). All that you and I do in seeking to extend this king's reign is to that end. Glory to God!

QUESTIONS FOR REFLECTION OR DISCUSSION

1. In your country, what does the idea of everyone being submitted to a single overarching ruler sound like? (Normal or despotic? [unlimited power over people, and often cruel and unfair])

2. Kingship and citizenship. When you first trusted in Christ, what was your understanding of the terms and conditions about being a disciple? (think about that, then read Luke 14:25-34 where the terms of discipleship are laid out).

3. Pick one of the images (crushed / rain/ licking the dust / gold). What struck you most about it in terms of you appreciating what Jesus has done for us, what he's done for you and me, or how *practically* he is to be honoured (we talked about the gold)?

4. In the original context David was handing over responsibility and praying for his successor. With God's specific help he also provided much in advance to help Solomon. So in closing, in your own area of leadership:

   a. As you pray for younger disciples and perhaps some leaders, what do you sense God saying about them, his plans for them?

   b. How are you going to communicate that with them?

   c. How are you helping them better understand and appreciate leadership and teamwork? (we've already noted in previous chapters the dangers of adopting an autocratic king-like leadership style).

AFTERWORD

THE BIBLE IS God's story, David one of his men, one of his leaders among a host of priests and prophets and kings, and lots of other men and women who point us to Christ. It is *his* story of salvation.

I trust that through these selected episodes in David's life you've been better able to understand what was happening at the time, how it shows our human frailties and our need of a greater king and how it points us to him.

Paul's words to Timothy, a younger leader God was shaping and forming seem apt here. May they be yours as the Lord continues to shape you for his glory, whatever your sphere and duration of service for the King.

> *Now to the King eternal, immortal, invisible, the only God, be honor and glory for ever and ever. Amen.*
>
> **1 Timothy 1:17**

APPENDIX A:
LOGOS AND RHEMA

GOD CAN AND does highlight things in Scripture to us, illuminate, shine his divine light on his written word, as well as bring specific verses to mind when we need them, but the word of God does not change into a 'rhema' word, a personal 'now' word to us,[51] 'a word that has become revelation'.[52] The *rhema* is not hidden within the 'logos'.

Some believers in charismatic circles sitting with their Bibles in front of them can end up waiting for a *rhema* word when they actually need to better learn how to pick up their knife and fork and dig into the Bible, use their mind, consider the context of the verse they are looking at, while asking God for *illumination*, for him to shine his light on the Scriptures they are reading or listening to. I believe that part of this problem comes from confusing teaching with prophecy and how they both work.

---

51. *The Pinnacle of the Temple,* Chuck Farah (*Logos* International, 1979) p 25-29
52. Pinnacle, p 51

The difference between teaching and a revelation

A 'teaching' (Greek *didache*) and a 'revelation' (Greek *apokalupto*) are clearly distinguished in 1 Corinthians 14:26. They involve us using different faculties.

1. Being given understanding about some Scripture or bringing a *teaching* involves first being given 'illumination': God shining his light on our hearts so we can grasp, perceive, comprehend the truth of what we are reading or hearing in the inspired and living Word of God. The word *illumination* comes from a Greek word ('*photizo*' – the root Greek word is '*phos*' from which we get 'light' and 'photo') meaning 'to illumine, to light up'. It is used in John 1:9 'the true *light* that gives light to everyone' (my italics). Jesus did it directly with the two on the road to Emmaus, opening up the Scriptures to them (Luke 24:13-35). While not connected with the reading of Scripture, Ephesians 1:18 says, 'that the eyes of your heart may be en*light*ened' (my italics).

   An Old Testament verse carrying the same idea is Psalm 119:18, 'Open my eyes, that I might see wonderful things in your law.' It's the clear acknowledgement and prayer that we need God the Holy Spirit to give us spiritual understanding as we read or listen to the Word of God. It's when God shines his light on the eyes of our heart, provides insight, opens our eyes. It's as if someone turns on the lights in a dark room; suddenly, we can see! For some, like Paul, who studied the Old Testament in depth for years before he could see spiritually, it's like the lights being turned on *in a library*. Same with the noted teacher Apollos who really knew the Old Testament (Acts 18). They have much to go over, much to re-examine. Little wonder some people end up in some backwater or isolated situation for a long period – necessary time to review and reconsider the Scriptures they know so well or revise preconceived notions about the faith.

   Paul wrote to Timothy, 'Reflect on what I am saying, for the Lord will give you insight into all this,' i.e. gain understanding as he reflected on Paul's words, which were to become part of

Holy Scripture (2 Timothy 2:7). That word translated 'insight' is also used by Paul when writing to the Ephesians, that they would read his letter so that they could understand his 'insight' into the mystery of Christ, that the Gentiles would join the Jews as heirs in Christ (Ephesians 3:4-6). It means 'putting things together in their understanding'; in other words, piecing it all together, getting the picture, joining the dots, as we might say.

It's when we're reading or listening to something in Scripture, something we may have read or heard many times before, and suddenly we 'get it'. When this happens the very first time, a veil over our heart is removed: we see the light of the gospel that displays the glory of Christ, turning to him. We see who Jesus is, turning from sin, putting our faith in him. Which is also why preaching is so important (2 Corinthians 3:12 – 4:6). And it's not simply a matter of grammar, of mental prowess, although the words of course need to make sense to us and not confuse us. If it were purely about grammar etc, then experts in the languages the Bible was originally written in would be the closest to God.

2. Being given a *revelation* (noun), for example a dream or vision or some other way of God speaking directly to us such as a gentle whisper, a light or cloud and a voice from heaven, or even a trance (see 1 Kings 19:12, Matthew 1:20, Luke 1:22, Luke 9:28-36, Acts 8:26-40, 9:1-10 & 10:10) does *not* come as a result of applying our minds as we study Scripture and asking God for *illumination*. It's something we *receive in our spirit* and which sometimes affects our whole being (consider the biblical examples above). I have a friend to whose bedroom window God sent a ball of light in the middle of the night. He experienced a tremendous sense of the Lord's presence as he hid under the bed covers. As he had been becoming more and more aware of God's presence over the weeks he was very aware it was a heavenly visitation of some sort (we recall that 'a light from heaven flashed around Paul' – Acts 9:3 – so there is a direct precedent). There were no lampposts or other lights outside his window. He's also a scientist by profession and less likely than some to get carried away by something unusual. It

was no deceiving angel. He came to faith not long afterwards and has been following Jesus for the last 35 years.

A *revelation* is also something we may then share *if we sense permission from God to do so* (Matthew 17:9). In the same way, the spirit of those who prophesy is also under their control: it's not a case of hysteria or 'I just had to speak that out, I couldn't help it'. God is a God of order, but not lacking power or desire to equip churches with lots of spiritual gifts (1 Corinthians 1:7; and 1 Corinthians 14, especially verse 32). For example, we receive a revelation and then later share it; when we share it, it is a prophecy, a spoken or written report to the other person or people, something uttered for the benefit of others. An excellent Old Testament example of this process is Nathan receiving a revelation and then reporting it to King David (2 Samuel 7). The revelation didn't come to David; it came to Nathan, who then shared it with David. To David it was a prophecy, a prophetic word. Paul speaks about this exact same process in 1 Corinthians chapter 14:26-32 in respect of a church gathering. A *revelation* (from *apokalupto*) is spontaneously received by someone 'sitting down' among the gathered congregation, i.e. the person is not standing up and speaking aloud at that time for all present to hear. But when and if they do speak out, i.e. share that revelation, it is then a prophecy, a report of what they sense God has revealed to them for the benefit of others in the congregation. The congregation can then weigh up, test, judge that report (1 Corinthians 14:29; 1 Thessalonians 5:19-22).

It's when we distinctly sense that God has spoken to us somehow, given us a *revelation* about something *apart from* when we are studying the Bible. Which is why it can happen anywhere. Reflect for a moment on *where* people were or what they were doing in the various biblical examples. It's as if God is 'pulling back the curtain' on something for us to see, revealing something to us that we would not otherwise know. Another useful image is of 'being given a song', of having something suddenly come to us. To underline the difference between a teaching (for which, like Bible study, we need *illumination*) and a prophecy etc (for which first we need a *revelation*), again consider the biblical examples already mentioned. Did Joseph have a dream in response to his request to better understand a Scripture? Did Zechariah have a vision of an angel as he pored over some Scripture, asking for illumination? Did an angel speak to Philip to give him understanding about some passage he was considering? Did Peter fall into a Spirit-induced trance in response to his focused reading of something in the Law or the Prophets? Did Nathan receive a revelation in the middle of the night to help him explain some Scripture or other? The answer to all these questions is no. What's recorded for us in all these instances is the process of being given a *revelation* by the Holy Spirit. Peter received a *revelation* that will have completely changed his view of Scripture, especially the right use of the Law of Moses; but it was a *revelation*, a dramatic starting point on a journey to help him realise that God accepts people from every nation. God graciously and powerfully built on this revelation by telling him to then go with some seemingly random men who had just arrived at the place he was staying at, and go with them to see the unconverted Roman soldier Cornelius, to whom God had also given a revelation. God then flooded that gathering of Gentiles at Cornelius' house with his Spirit, interrupting Peter's preaching. Which should also tell us that it was not only a historically important moment in the development of the Church in accepting Gentiles, it was the outworking of God's plan to bless all nations, and an example of God's promise to pour out his Spirit on all in the last days – the time from Jesus' ascension *to his return* – and that God is quite willing to interrupt our meetings by the influence of his Spirit and introduce other gifts into the mix, yet without minimising the importance of evangelistic preaching.

God very well might reveal something specific to someone to share *apart from* or *in addition to* their study of the Bible or indeed their preaching, but in that instance it would be teaching with, e.g. prophecy added in; teaching with some other word or other added. It is a *revelation* God has given the person *in addition to* the *teaching* they brought, the sermon they preached, the message they shared (usually with a fair amount of study with *illumination* beforehand).

It is the same God, the same Holy Spirit at work revealing things to the person, but one is a *teaching* (for which we first need *illumination*), the other a *revelation*. Two different things. I hope I'm making this clear. As noted in chapter 13, Daniel 9 and 10 are instructive in this matter in terms of distinguishing between on the one hand being given understanding about some Scripture or some teaching from Scripture (9:2), and a revelation on the other (10:1).

Logos and rhema

The argument for *logos* meaning the whole of Scripture or the written word of God, and *rhema* being an inspired, specific, spoken word from within it, can be traced back to the book, *From the Pinnacle of the Temple* (1979) by Chuck Farah. There may be another earlier development someone knows of. Farah may have leaned on William Vine's *Expository Dictionary of New Testament Words* first published in 1940. It was for many years a helpful resource, especially for those who hadn't studied any of the biblical languages. It states, 'The significance of *rhema* (as distinct from *logos*), is exemplified in the injunction to take 'the sword of the Spirit, which is the word of God' (Ephesians 6:17); here the reference is not to the whole Bible as such, but to the individual scripture which the Spirit brings to our remembrance for use in time of need, a prerequisite being the regular storing of the mind with Scripture.'[53]

Farah argues that the *logos-rhema* distinction is a theological construct, i.e. a tool or device to help us better understand and communicate matters about the faith. He states that the apostle John often uses *logos* to mean the universal and eternal, the word of God, i.e. Christ (e.g. John 1:1 and 1:14). And since *rhema* is sometimes used to mean a 'now' word, a personal word for the moment, a specific word for a specific person, if you contrast *logos* and *rhema* then you can use it as 'a teaching tool that helps us to understand *the difference between*

---

53. *An Expository Dictionary of New Testament Words.* W.E. Vine (Fleming H. Revell, NJ, 1940), p 230

a general and a particular word of the Lord.[54] Just as Vine suggests. But as Farah readily admits, 'the Scriptures…do not teach a clear and unambiguous distinction between these two words.'[55] He states that the two words are used interchangeably in the Bible, 'except in John'.[56] The problem is, that is simply incorrect: they are used interchangeably in John as well, with a couple of notable uses at the start of John that point to the deity of our wonderful Saviour.

1. *Logos* (pronounced in the original, 'log-os') appears over 300 times in the New Testament and can be used to describe someone speaking (a speech or a report or a statement), or an idea or reasoning expressed by words. It can also be used in a weighty theological sense, depending on the context, as in John 1:1 and 1:14 (the *logos*, the pre-existing Word became flesh). *Logos* is also used by the woman at the well in her 'testimony' (the 'logon' [from *logos*] of the woman) afterwards to her village. It was her spoken word, her testimony, her report (John 4:39). When Jesus healed an official's son simply by uttering a word, 'Go, your son will live' (4:50), it states that the man believed the specific 'word' Jesus spoke to him. And the Greek used in that sentence? *Logos,* not *rhema.* You might argue that this is the written record, the Scriptures, so these examples and Jesus' words are all *logos,* not *rhema.* But as we'll see, from the Bible you cannot argue that *logos* equals the written word of God, and that *rhema* equals the spoken or inspired word of God.

   When Jesus was in Jerusalem teaching, some Jews asked: "What did he mean (literally, 'what is the "word" – *logos*') when he said, 'You will look for me, but you will not find me'" (John 7:36). In other words, what did Jesus means by the things, the *logos,* he said. Of importance is John 12:48 where both *logos* and *rhema* are used very close to each other: 'There is a judge for the one who rejects me and does not accept my words (*rhema*); the very words (*logos*) I have spoken will condemn them at the last day.' Finally consider the specific spoken words by the Jewish leaders to Pilate: 'If you let

---

54. p 51 (my emphasis)
55. p 50
56. p 51

this man go, you are no friend of Caesar. Anyone who claims to be a king opposes Caesar' (John 19:12). 'When Pilate heard 'this' (logon [plural of *logos*], i.e. the word*s* of the Jewish leaders), he brought Jesus out' (John 19:13). Pilate was referring to the specific spoken words of the Jewish leaders.

As importantly, while *logos* is used in John 1:1, 14 and Revelation 19:13 to refer to Jesus the 'Word of God', it is not used in the New Testament to refer directly to the 'Scriptures', i.e. the written word of God. A different word is used for that (see the section below *The written word of God.*) As we've seen, *logos* has a wide range of usage, including referring to the word of God, from which we can sometimes take to mean the Scriptures. For example, Jesus said, 'If he called them "gods," to whom the word (*logos*) of God came – and the Scripture cannot be set aside – what about the one....(John 10:35). Jesus often said, 'It is written' and 'Have you never read?' by which he was of course referring to the Old Testament writings (Luke 24:44). He said he had come to 'fulfil the law'. The eternal and living Word of God, the Lord Jesus, came to fulfil the writings, the written word of God. Hallelujah. Jesus quoted a Scripture in Isaiah 29 when he told some Pharisees, 'You have let go of the commands of God and are holding onto human traditions' (Mark 7:8).

As Farah rightly points out, *logos* is used by the other New Testament writers in a variety of ways. Consider Paul's letter to the Ephesians: 'Do not let any unwholesome talk (*logos*) come out of your mouths' (4:29), and 'Pray also for me, that whenever I speak, words (*logos*) may be given me so that I will fearlessly make known the mystery of the gospel' (6:19). In Acts, *logos* often refers to the gospel (the 'word of the Lord' or 'the word of God') but it's also used in other situations, e.g. Ananias fell down dead when he heard Peter's words (*logos* plural) – Acts 5:5. Some of us would have definitely say that it was a *rhema* word, a now or special word Peter had for Ananias. But the word *logos* does not carry any weight in the sentence, i.e. it's not central to understanding the sentence or passage. It's the content of his words that were important. And consider the word used for 'the word/message of wisdom' and 'the word/message of knowledge', both spiritual gifts involving people *speaking* out something God has revealed to them (1 Corinthians 12:8). You guessed it: *logos*.

As with John 12:48, we see *logos* and *rhema* being used by Peter in his first letter to refer to 'the word of God' and 'the word of the Lord': 'For you have been born again, not of perishable seed, but of imperishable, through the living and enduring word (*logos*) of God. For "All people are like grass...but the word (*rhema*) of the Lord endures forever." And this was the word (*rhema*) that was preached to you' (1 Peter 1:23-25). Peter was not referring to some specific *rhema* word he took from the written *logos* of God (in his context the Old Testament) because a. He uses *rhema* to refer to the enduring *word* of the Lord (the same word for 'enduring' or 'abiding' is also used before the enduring *logos* of God, i.e. one and same thing); and b. He was writing to believers scattered across hundreds of square miles (there's no evidence to suggest that by 'this was the *rhema* that was preached to you' he was referring to some specific spoken sermon they had all heard.) He was using *logos* and *rhema* interchangeably to refer to the enduring word of God / word of the Lord.

2. *Rhema* (pronounced in the original 'ray-mah') appears 70 times in the New Testament and means a thing spoken, a word or saying of any kind, quite often a specific word or utterance; or words about an event or thing or object (as in 2 Corinthians 13:1). It is never used to refer to some special word of revelation. As we've seen, and as Vine above cites, *rhema* is indeed used to describe the sword of the Spirit, i.e. the word of God (Ephesians 6:17). And 'every word (*rhema*) that comes from the mouth of God' (Matthew 4:4). But not only is *rhema* used to refer to specific human speech, especially by people, it is also sometimes used to mean the more general, which a saying or expression of any kind must necessarily include. For example, Jesus said, "Whoever belongs to God hears what God 'says' (his words – *rhema*)..." (John 8:47). Are we going to argue that Jesus was excluding the Scriptures in that sentence or context,

or by *rhema* he was referring to some specific words from Scripture or 'now' words that are inspired and that the Scriptures are not? Peter exclaimed, "You [Jesus] have the 'words' (*rhema* in plural) of eternal life!" (John 6:68). Referring to the Church, Paul wrote, "... to make her holy, cleansing her by the washing with water through the 'word' (again, from *rhema*) (Ephesians 5:26).

What Paul is getting at in Ephesians 6:17 and what is recorded for us in Matthew 4 is quoting the word of God as a sword – three examples in Matthew 4 about *speaking out* words, Bible verses, to quickly rebut Satan. Christ is our example. We are commanded to do the same by memorising Scripture (Psalm 119:11) and trusting that the Holy Spirit will bring those words to mind, shine his light on specific words of Scripture that will then help us defeat Satan, and also sin, especially during trials in which we not only need perseverance but wisdom. God is unchanging and good and not a deceiver (James 1:1-18).

It's all part of submitting to God and resisting the devil (James 4:7), which when put in context of the surrounding verses involves us not being friends with the world by arguing with each other because we selfishly want this and that from God so we can spend money on our pleasures. If we try and resist the devil when we are not submitted to God, we will soon fall flat on our faces or get horribly exposed to the enemy who can see clearly that we have no authority due to not being under authority. The order is submission to God then resisting the devil.

I was once in a small group of young people who had pulled away from the main gathering at a youth retreat late one evening. Some of those present started rebuking the devil. One of them suddenly began to get suffocated, gasping for breath. It did not take a genius to work out that an evil spirit had been permitted to harass or oppress her. A few little lambs had left the safety of the flock and had decided to shout abuse at the wolves encircling the field. A more experienced believer, a woman, then came into the room, and gently placing one hand on the young woman's throat simply said, 'Satan, I bind you in Jesus' name.' She was immediately released, let out a gasp of air. At the time it was short and dramatic. Tails between our legs, we went to bed, just as the main youth leader ordered. And we had all learned an important lesson.

In Ephesians, Paul was using the image of the Roman soldier to illustrate the cutting and thrusting edge of the sharpness of God's word. It is not only effective against sin and the Tempter, it also cuts to the heart, divides between soul and spirit. The *logos* of God is alive and active and exposes the attitudes and thoughts of the human heart (Hebrews 4:12). When we hear his voice, God speaking to us as we read Scripture or in some other way, we are not to harden our hearts but instead combine our hearing with faith – believe and obey God and not be like those who fell in the desert (Hebrews 3:1 – 4:13).

A problem for some, not for others

In conservative evangelical churches none of this is really an issue, as it's not the language of faith they use to describe such things. And if you don't know any Greek then it may not be an issue. At the same time, those who have studied Greek may cringe when they hear blanket statements about *logos* and *rhema* as they double check their Greek New Testament and think (or blog or write), 'Mmm, that's not true'.

So what's going on?

Farah is arguing for a *logos-rhema* distinction and using it as a theological tool, language that may help us better understand and explain spiritual matters, when something we've read in Scripture becomes fresh to us or is brought to mind by the Spirit. But as Farah clearly agrees, the use of both *logos* and *rhema* in the New Testament depends on the immediate context, which is why they are used in a variety of ways. Same with any word (think of the possible meanings of 'trunk' when driving a family car on safari with elephants and trees!) As we've seen, John does use *logos* to refer to Christ, the pre-existent Word, in his account of the gospel (John 1:1 and 1:14), but forging a New Testament theological tool on the basis of how one word is *sometimes* used in a single book of the Bible may cause trouble for some people further down the line. Even if it was often used that way it's still fraught with danger.

It may help people not to jump to conclusions when they read something written in the Bible, as in the classic case of a new believer reading in one scripture 'Judas hanged himself' (Matthew 23:5) and then the next 'Now that you know these things, you will be blessed if you do them' (John 13:17) and then wondering if he/she should end it all (or jump off a cliff as Satan tempted Jesus with when misquoting Psalm 91 – Luke 4:10). But we don't need a *logos-rhema* tool to tell us this is just wrong; we need divine *illumination* as we read, God's flashlight/torch on our thinking, a growing knowledge of the breadth of God's Word, memorising it, so that we can recognise misquotes for what they really are: deception, or ignorance. Jesus cited three specific verses from Deuteronomy in his encounter with the Tempter in the desert (Matthew 4). As with Jesus in his humanity, there were no shortcuts: he will have memorised these. As we've seen, as we do this too, being in submission to God, the Holy Spirit will graciously bring to mind specific Scriptures when we most need them; he will teach and remind us of the things God has spoken to us before (John 14:26).

Farah claims that using *logos-rhema* does not need 'complete scriptural endorsement.'[57] But you can't build a trustworthy tool by using two words in the Bible to mean something when it does not fit with how those words are used the Bible. That tool can eventually become an unreliable instrument, especially in immature, or worse, deceptive hands. Farah does offer a word of caution,[58] stating that the tool is not a doctrine. But in some circles it has become just that. Ironically, a good number of teachers, including those in the 'word of faith' movement whose teaching Farah was challenging in the same book, have used his *logos-rhema* tool to promote their doctrines, confusing 'teaching' with 'revelation,' using the *rhema* argument to claim biblical verses mean something the context does not teach.

---

57. p 50
58. p 49

Farah's motive

To be fair, Farah was trying to explain why some people had not been physically healed. Some people had wrongly taken for themselves some spoken words that were actually intended for others, i.e. the word received or believed, or that had been preached or shared, had been a *rhema* word, a 'now word', but it was for someone else, not them. It became *rhema* for the other person, but remained *logos* for them. 'Confession', was not after all, 'possession'; while encouraging greater faith, you could not just 'name and claim it.' For example, he uses the story of Jesus' interaction with John and Peter in John 21 to emphasise his point. He argues that Jesus was saying in his reply to Peter when he asked, 'What about him?' (i.e. John), 'I have a *rhema* for you, and I have *rhema* for John, but the *rhema* I have for John is none of your business'.[59] The word *rhema* is not anywhere in that passage, and the word *logos* is used to describe the rumour, the words the *disciples* used about the matter afterwards. As a tool, *logos* vs. *rhema can* be used to illustrate that Jesus' words to someone else are not really any of our business: we must follow him. *But we don't need logos vs rhema to try and explain that: the context tells us.* (some sanctified common sense does not hurt in some instances either.)

As mentioned, Farah relies largely on the gospel according to John for his *logos-rhema* distinction argument and tool, and I appreciate his heart in seeking to combat some of the excesses in the charismatic movement he was seeing at the time (and which still exist), and the pain caused (he dedicates the book to those 'for whom a faith-formula has not worked'), but in trying to explain what went wrong he has perhaps created a tool some teachers have since gone on to make an important doctrine. Some have even added it to their list of doctrines that helps earn them lots of money (prosperity teaching / the prosperity gospel.)

The biblical use of both *logos* and *rhema* (especially in John 12:48 and 1 Peter 1:23-25 – see above) only underlines the fact that we cannot neatly divide the words up to create a solid theological tool, as attractive or helpful as that seems, because it is not consistent with Scripture itself. And it's so easily distorted. *Rhema* can end up topping

---

59. p 30

logos: a so called 'revelation' can supersede the plain meaning of the biblical text in front of us, especially if the person does not know their Bible. It may be a helpful illustration, but we would be better off not using Greek words like *logos* and *rhema*.

In a moment we'll consider a different couple of illustrations that may more accurately reflect the biblical words used to describe such processes, perhaps a better way of explaining how it is that God seems to graciously highlight things to us in his Word, the Bible, remind of us things we've read when we need them, *and* how he can break into our and others' lives by giving us a *revelation*, i.e. a dream, vision or trance, or some word we may later end up sharing with others.

None of us is immune to getting it wrong, mishearing something we think God has promised us, whether we call it a *rhema* word or not. We cannot take something God has said to someone else and take it for ourselves if God has not made that clear to us. Unless it's a general principle in the Bible, if we take a word God has highlighted to us and make it a general word or principle, we will get into trouble. This is what Farah was trying to achieve using his general vs specific, *logos* vs *rhema* argument. And as he clearly points out, there are things we'll never understand this side of eternity; some people do not get healed, and it's not their fault, it's often not a lack of faith. It's why Lamentations (national trauma) and Job (personal trauma) are in the Bible for us to help us slowly build a theology of suffering which involves acknowledging mystery and unanswered questions, not just a theology of healing. If there is no suffering now, then we don't need Job or Lamentations, or any other verses that clearly speak of suffering, as well as accounts of sick people not being healed. For example, Paul left Trophimus 'sick, weak' in Miletus (2 Timothy 4:20) with no suggestion of a lack of faith on Paul or Trophimus' part. The same word for sick or weak is used many times in the gospel to refer to sick people (Matthew 10:8; Mark 6:56; Luke 4:40; John 4:46 – which as we've seen Jesus healed with a logos). At the same time, some of us also need to see far more examples of healing in practice, i.e. the kingdom of God being manifested in the form of miracles such as gifts of healing. Having a theology that includes physical healing today is one thing; seeing it in practice is another (1 Corinthians 12:9). The truth is we need both: doctrine *and* experience.

Barth and neo-orthodoxy

When I first heard the *logos-rhema* teaching it seemed to smell a bit Barth-like, theologian Karl Barth (1886-1968), to be precise. As well as the good things Barth wrote and did, he believed that the Bible itself was *not* revelation, not *itself* the Word of God: 'When divine revelation meets us and we respond in faith and obedience, the Bible *becomes* the Word of God;[60] 'The Bible is God's Word so far as God lets it be his Word'.[61] In other words, you need revelation *for it to become the word of God to you*, something alive. But the Bible *is* the Word of God, God's special revelation, his inspired Word (as opposed to general revelation, God revealing himself through creation – Romans 1:20). It's alive and inerrant in it's original writings. Yes, we need the Holy's Spirit's light (illumination) in order to understand it, but it does *not* become the word of God as we read it. Neither does *logos* become *rhema*[62] which is where we can get into trouble. As we've seen, *logos*, word, has all sorts of uses in the Bible.

The example of misusing proverbs

Farah also mentions the misuse of the biblical proverbs, taking them as promises in every situation, of people using them to defend 'word of faith' teaching. He's spot on. But ironically, here again the *logos-rhema* tool can be used to distort things and create rules and spiritual laws that apply in all situations. ('Hardly Farah's fault' someone might argue. But like I say, in all this it might be better distinguishing between *teaching* [for which we need *illumination* as we engage our intellect in studying or hearing or recalling Scripture] and *revelation*; the difference between using a knife and fork and using a pick/plectrum.)

---

60. Barth quoted in p98 of volume 1 of *Integrative Theology* by G. Lewis and B. Demarest (Zondervan, 1996)
61. Evangelical Dictionary of Theology (2nd ed). Edited by Walter Elwell (Baker Academic, 2001) p820.
62. *Pinnacle*, p28

For instance, preacher X claims that's he's had a *rhema* word about some proverb and then proceeds to turn it into a law, a now word he's received, and something for everyone to get hold of. 'God gave me the key to this verse! It came alive to me!' It can then become a rule, a promise for all times and situations, a spiritual cause and effect law. But the proverbs are not promises true for every person and situation – they are principles that are situation-specific. The are proverbial wisdom, maxims about how life works, wisdom for the people of God about how to live, and which ultimately point us to Christ, the Wisdom of God, who calls out to us. It is *Him* we should fear (Proverbs chapters 1 and 8).

God will sometimes highlight a proverb (as he does in illuminating other verses or passages to us, as we've seen), explaining something that has happened in a situation we're in, i.e. a life-principle at work. But they are not true in every situation. For example, it's generally true that 'all hard work brings a profit' (14:23), but that's not true in every situation, it's not a promise for every circumstance. For example, you've worked hard and a world-wide pandemic wipes out your business, or someone steals your money, or your farm you've worked hard on gets flooded. To emphasis the nature of how proverbs work, a superb example is Proverbs 26 verses 4 & 5 – back to back verses which contradict each other. Try taking them as promises at the same time! They underline the same point: it depends on the circumstances, in this case the particular situation and which particular fool you are dealing with. If you want a really helpful little book on Proverbs and how they work, grab a copy of *How to Read Proverbs* by Tremper Longman III.

Does it matter?

As mentioned, for some in the charismatic wing of the Church who know their Bibles the *logos-rhema* tool does not present a problem. They have not turned it into a doctrine; they may find it helpful for distinguishing between those times a specific word is highlighted to them or brought to mind by the Spirit just when they need it. They may feel that any disagreement over the whole *logos-rhema* thing is splitting hairs, arguing over mere words – semantics. They can use it as a tool and not get into any bother. But as one Pentecostal pastor friend told me, 'It's an area where cliche can turn into lazy theology which in turn can turn into poor praxis.'

By using *logos* to refer to the written Word of God, the Scriptures, there is a danger in some circles, of inadvertently downgrading the Bible to a dead document that needs 'a revelation' or a *rhema* moment or word for it to become alive or inspired. *Logos* becomes limited to the written word, and *rhema* the inspired, spoken word. But we've seen that the use of those two words used in the Bible do not support this. And besides, the Scriptures are 'breathed out', i.e. inspired by God! (2 Timothy 3:16). And Jesus said we are to come to him: the writings are supposed to lead us to him (John 5:37-40).

The written word of God

The word most commonly used in the New Testament to refer to the written word of God, is 'graphe' (pronounced 'grah-<u>fay</u>') and it means 'sacred writing' or 'scripture'. Less commonly used is 'gramma' meaning 'letter' or 'document' e.g. 'Take your bill' (Like 16:6). Both come from the Greek verb 'grapho' meaning 'to write', as in Matthew 4:4 'It is written', or when the Roman soldiers who crucified Jesus placed the 'written' sign, 'This is Jesus, the King of the Jews' (Matthew 27:37). Paul refers to the Scriptures as the sacred 'writings', the holy Scriptures, the Old Testament that Timothy had known since childhood (2 timothy 3:15). 'Every graphe (Scripture) is God-breathed and is useful for *teaching* etc' (2 Timothy 3:16 – my emphasis to underline the fact again that *teaching* is directly connected with Scripture, while prophecy etc is directly connected with *revelation*). Interestingly, in 2 Timothy 4:2 where it says, 'Preach the word', it's not *graphe* that is used but *logos*. Putting it in context of what's come before it, that 'word' is the message about Christ, the message of salvation *that we get wisdom about from God's breathed-out graphe, the Scriptures*. Which is actually central. Using the Bible, the written word of God, without looking and pointing responsibly in context to Jesus the Living Word is using it for something other than which God commanded. As should be obvious, that's a deadly serious matter. What if God were to summon you or me tonight and ask, 'Explain to me why you used my Word to preach and teach on things without focusing on my Son?' The priority is the Master, not money; servanthood, not spelling out principles for 'success.' Is that what the apostle Paul preached?

The word of faith

The context of Romans 10:5-18 (especially v 8 'the word of faith, which we preach') is a righteousness that is by faith, not by Jewish law. The Jews needed to hear the message about Christ, which is why they needed preachers, which is why preachers like Paul and others needed to be sent. Beautiful feet bringing the good news. Faith did not come, does not come, by law or works, but by hearing the word, the *rhema* of Christ. But the Jews were stubborn (v21). The passage is littered with not only *rhema* but direct quotes from the Old Testament. While a different book of the Bible, when we compare it for a moment with Paul's emphasis on preaching the good news in 2 Timothy 4:2 where he uses *logos*, the surrounding and especially the immediate context around 2 Timothy 4:2 is about Scripture. My point is that in both passages *rhema* and *logos* are used in connection with Scripture and the importance of preaching so that people will be saved or instructed in the faith. Timothy was to do the work of an evangelist (2 Timothy 4:5). The logos / rhema of God endures for ever. It's a case of both/and, not either/or.

To recap

Terms, the words and phrases we use to explain things, can become important. God can and does highlight things to us in his Word (the Scriptures). We see the tremendous example of our Lord combating Satan with specific words of Scripture (Luke 4). All believers will have experienced some verse or other really sticking out to them, of God underlining something. 'God really spoke to me!' we say. Amazing! Yet if we are reading or listening to the Bible or sound preaching, *then God is also speaking to us right there and then, i.e. now.* It's not that the Scriptures are stale and need freshening up, or that *logos* needs to become the *rhema* for us. It's more than we need light, illumination, to be given understanding.

If the Word of God means nothing to us, it may mean that our ears need circumcised! Not a matter of the word of God needing to become alive, but for our ears to be opened. Jeremiah 6:10 says, 'To whom can I speak and give warning? Who will listen to me? Their ears are closed so they cannot hear. The word of the LORD is offensive to them; they find no pleasure in it' (Jeremiah 6:10, 'closed'… literally 'uncircumcised ears').

What's happening in these situations is that the Holy Spirit has given us fresh insight and helped us see where and how the written Word of God applies to our specific circumstances at that time, whether personal, family, church or society. And it's incredible and encourages us in our faith. A good doctor knows which particular medicine to meet our physical needs; our Father and Heavenly Physician and Creator knows not only that, but which particular passage of Scripture to meet our spiritual needs, for we do not live on bread alone. Good shepherds, i.e. elders/pastors have a good idea of which part of the Holy Scriptures apply to the various pastoral needs they are called to minister to. And then there are the other gifts of that same Holy Spirit to enable a church to be blessed and be a blessing. To repeat: what we need is the Spirit's *illumination* as we read and search the Scriptures; yes, for God to reveal things to us, but not '*a revelation*' or a '*rhema word*' as such, as that's a different thing.

Another, better way of describing the difference

When teaching about the nature of prophecy I've sometimes used the image of a 'microscope' versus a 'telescope' to differentiate between what has been called 'forthtelling' (speaking into a person's situation at that time, like a microscope on something in their life and circumstances) and 'foretelling' (predicting the future, like a telescope looking into the distance). Most prophecy is forthtelling. People have found the illustration helpful.

In the same way, instead of using a *logos* word versus a *rhema* word, here are some images that I've already touched on that:

1. Better reflect the difference between those moments when God's Spirit gives *illumination* as we read or listen to the Bible, or recall some verse, and those times when he provides a *revelation* in the form of a dream or vision etc or some other clear word.

2. More accurately reflect the use of both the words *illumination* and *revelation* in the biblical contexts we've been discussing.

For *illumination*: the image of a **flashlight** or **torch** or **lightbulb** or a **spotlight** – God shining his light on some Scripture or other, which as we've seen can happen when we're on our own with the Bible, or when the Spirit brings some Scripture to mind just when we need it, or when someone is preaching or bringing a *teaching*.

For a *revelation*: when **a song suddenly comes to us** or when **the curtain is pulled back** (think of a play in a theatre) for us to see something behind the scenes that is happening or is going to happen. This can lead to someone sharing it in the form of a *prophecy*.

A **Spotlight** versus a **Curtain** being drawn back. **Flashlight** vs a **Song**. Take your pick of pairings. You may be able to think of some other useful images.

Our part is picking up our knives and forks, getting into the living Word of God, and asking the Holy Spirit to give us *illumination*, fresh insight, and if we are gifted to teach, then to bring a *teaching* as God leads us. **And** pursuing God for the gifts of his Spirit, especially *prophecy* etc, each utterance for which we first need a *revelation*. We need both these dynamics for the health and mission of the Church. More, not less of the Spirit and his gifts (see appendix B). The Lord will surely help us if we ask him.

APPENDIX B:
MORE OR LESS OF THE SPIRIT?

THE FILLING OF the Spirit is also connected with spiritual songs and words.[63] It's why the immature but gifted church in Corinth needed to have some sort of order; not *less* of the Spirit and his work among them, but greater maturity in how they understood and handled things in their meetings together since it was common for one person to share a psalm, another *a teaching*, and yet another to bring *a revelation*, etc; different elements, but from the same Holy Spirit (1 Corinthians 14: 3 & 26). And these different elements need a proper sense of order, e.g. two or at the most three prophesying in turn. I've only experienced this once in a meeting: two tongues with interpretation in a row (equal to prophecy – 1 Corinthians 14:5). By the end of the minutes during which they were shared, half the people

---

63. For example, Mary's song (Luke 1) when she met her relative Elizabeth; also Ephesians 5:18-20 where it says, '...go on being filled with the Spirit... speaking to one another with psalms, hymns, and songs from the Spirit. Sing and make music from your heart to the Lord.'
Many commentators and church leaders who hold to a dynamic filling of the Spirit and tongues and other spiritual gifts, believe 'spiritual songs' are inspired songs given in the moment. It might involve also musical accompaniment, spontaneous playing which must involves a previously acquired baseline level of skill. Hence why David's plans for the temple included prophetic singers who had been trained (1 Chronicles 25:1). How much more then New Testament Christian living no longer restricted to a single physical building but one being built all over the world in cities and local communities by the Lord with himself as the chief cornerstone (Ephesians 2:19-22).

in the room were on the floor in awe of God, such was the sense of his presence.

If we don't have any sort of order, things can get confusing. Before I got up to preach at one young church, no less than twelve prophecies were shared at the meeting. It was also clear that not everything people were sharing were words of prophecy; some were more words of encouragement. Such encouragement in the use of the gifts was and is good; they just needed a sense of order as things could get overloaded, confused. As with the church in Corinth, it's not that these things should be stamped out as being divisive or disruptive, in favour of a scripted meeting that is never deviated from.

In his first letter to the Corinthians, Paul was underlining the importance of order: *cutting down* not *cutting out* certain practices, bringing some order. Two or at the most three people in a row should speak out in tongues in hope of someone being given the interpretation (1 Corinthians 14:27). It's easier to rule certain things completely out due to fear or ignorance, but it does not sit with Paul's counsel to the immature Corinthian church. There was plenty of fire in their life and in their meetings. But the fire needed to be tended, not extinguished; prophetic words encouraged and tested, not ruled out or consigned to something a preacher might sometimes sense during preaching (1 Thessalonians 5:19-20; note the context has nothing to do with preaching).

A helpful example of this early on in the Pentecostal movement (birthed in Wales in 1904) is the visit of pastor Donald Gee to Australia during 1928. Having been invited to preach in various parts of the country to lots of Pentecostal assemblies that had sprung up there, God gave him a dream the night before he set sail from the U.K. In the dream he was busy shovelling coal in the boiler room of a big ocean liner – the engine was throbbing with power. But suddenly realising that no one was on the bridge helping steer the great ship, he rushed upstairs and managed to turn the liner away from some rocks it was about to crash into.

When he arrived in Australia by ship some weeks later, he found the Pentecostal assemblies throbbing with life and power: '...plenty of evangelistic fire but there was an over-emphasis on the spectacular and the miraculous, and the good ship was headed for the rocks.'[64] Through the dream, it was clear God had graciously prepared him for what was ahead and so helped Donald strengthen that branch of his, God's Church, and helped prevent the fledgling movement from crashing onto the rocks. Gee developed into an excellent itinerant Bible teacher, able to help equip the saints by making difficult subjects easier to understand, especially in the area of spiritual gifts. He was instrumental in helping bring understanding and order – and critically, *balance* – but realised the fire must be kept burning so that the ship kept moving. Everyone needs to be on fire.

Movements involve mess. New births are not clean and tidy affairs. Adopting children into an existing family is also not some smooth affair – everyone has to adjust. Do we want new life with its glorious mess, or to die slowly having slowly extinguished life (maybe over many decades) out of fear or lack of understanding and experience? When compared to Paul's litmus test of *content* (a hymn, a message in tongues, interpretation of tongues, a teaching, a revelation, some knowledge, a prophecy – 1 Corinthians 14:3 & 26), how do our meetings compare? When compared to Paul's litmus test in terms of *order* (not cutting things out), how do our meetings compare? These are sobering questions. Yet we have a gracious Father and Shepherd who is only too eager to instruct us if we let him. That may involve having a conversation with someone who knows more about this area of ministry than we do. But a wise person seeks advice :) (Proverbs 15:32-33).

The same goes for someone who better understands what it means to receive a revelation, but needs some help to better use their knife and fork. Of central importance is how we view the filling of the Spirit. If we see the book of Acts as more descriptive (not all for today), then we will not see evidence of such things among us. We don't believe it is for today; we don't believe God wants to do such things in and through us today. But if we see Acts as more normative (still for today) then we will be encouraged to seek God for such things now. Let's remember

---

64. *Seven Pentecostal Pioneers* by Colin Whittaker (Marshall Pickering, London: 1986) p 92-93.

that Paul's letters came *after* the events described in Acts: they include instruction about how to seek and handle all manner of spiritual gifts, the experiences of believers being written out for us in Acts.

A word of encouragement and challenge

Let me encourage you. Few of us are called to be teachers (James 3:1) but all can receive the power of the Spirit, a mighty filling. This also opens the door to receive revelations and all that can develop from that. In Scripture, wherever we see the activity and work of the Spirit we see these things, as well as evangelism and mission. And it's an ongoing filling, especially when we need it for some type of service or situation. It's no mistake that those who attest to a post-conversion encounter of the Holy Spirit also speak of other spiritual gifts and miraculous events happening in their circles. It tends to open the door to other spiritual gifts and phenomena.

I remember listening to a message by Donald Campbell speaking about the Lewis Revival of 1951 of the northwest coast of Scotland. He clearly stated that the revival did not come to Barvas, because the people there were opposed to the teaching about being baptised, i.e. filled, with the Holy Spirit as a definite post-conversion experience. Sobering stuff.

That some charismatic people or groups are unstable does not invalidate their experience or testimony. In such cases what's needed is more skill with the knife and fork, getting into the Word and rightly applying it, *including how spiritual gifts should be used and the principles for how to interpret things like dreams etc.* In other words, better and more biblical teaching as well as pursuing the God of the miraculous. And everything, including prophesies must be tested and not simply dismissed (1 Thessalonians 5:19: 'despised'). If they don't come to pass or lead us away from the Lord, then they didn't come from God.[65]

---

65. The start of Deuteronomy chapter 13 and end of chapter 18, while addressing Old Testament prophets and prophecy where what they said was the Word of God (not so today), is helpful in this matter. Which is why everything today is still to be weighed up, and accepted if accurate, fulfilled, leading to encouragement etc, but not treated as *the* Word of God, otherwise people making errors would need to be dealt with in the same way as under the Old Covenant, i.e. put to death (!)

The opposite situation is where a church is well taught, but lacking spiritual power; great Bible teaching, but few signs of the miraculous. That Word and Spirit dynamic, that balance, is well worth pursuing. Indeed it is commanded: 'Let the Word of Christ dwell in you richly' (Colossians 3:16) and 'Be filled with the Spirit' (Ephesians 5:18). Not either / or. What do we think being filled with the Spirit meant to those in Acts? Their stories tell us. It was something that happened to them, and they knew it, felt it. Just as you know that you've been baptised (immersed) with water, i.e. you're wet and no one can tell you otherwise, so too when you are immersed in the Spirit you know it, and no one can tell you otherwise. Have you been filled with the Holy Spirit? Is it something that has happened to you?

It is why Christ gives teachers *and* prophets, teaching *and* prophesy. Such gifts and individuals who minister in this way more frequently, are given by Christ to help equip the saints in the same way that the vital role an evangelist can fulfil is in not simply preaching the gospel but equipping the saints in their own lives so they can better love and reach those around them. In this way, the whole body grows as each part does its work (Ephesians 4:11-16). The charismatic and conservative wings of the Church can actually learn from each other; one is often better at handling the Scriptures, the other a wider range of the gifts of the Spirit and how they operate in practice.

A helpful analogy I've used on many occasions is that of an amphibious vehicle. If the land and its hills, valleys, forests, deserts and wetlands, etc are like the various genres of the Bible and understanding and applying them, then the water is the Holy Spirit and his gifts we also need to become familiar with. (Yes, I know we get rivers running through the land but that might make the analogy a little complex; it's just an analogy:). Like amphibious vehicles, churches need to *understand* and *experience* both the land and the water, becoming knowledgeable and confident in both, which is where solid teachers and prophets come in, as at Antioch (Acts 13:1-2). Is your fellowship or group more comfortable on land or water? Maybe your people are used to both.

Meditating on the analogy further for a moment, it's interesting when we consider the success and sometimes the failure of churches focused largely on only one of these. A church which concentrates mostly on staying on the water (the Holy Spirit and his gifts) can be spectacular and yield quick results – quite the ride! But it is also in danger of taking on water and quickly sinking because it lacks the safety and stability of the land. Consider Donald Gee's visit to Australia mentioned earlier.

On the other hand, a church that concentrates largely on staying on land (preaching and teaching etc) will be stable. But it is in danger of slowing down or slowly drying up and failing to advance the gospel as it might – few signs of the miraculous and lacking energy in evangelism.

As someone once said, "All Spirit and you can blow up; all Word and you can dry up. Engage fully with both and you (better) grow up." May the Lord, who is Sovereign, be gracious to you and bring you whatever your need at this hour, whether personally or in your church.

In the case of the water, I personally had no understanding of who the Holy Spirit was or what he did when I first encountered Christ. I had repented and Jesus had come into my life. I was very sure of that. Twenty minutes later, the same young man who had earlier led me in prayer to receive the Saviour then prayed for me and laid hands on me. My body was suddenly flooded with power and I began to shake and then speak in another language (tongues) as we were praying aloud at the same time. I was pretty shocked and excited, so was the guy praying for me. He already spoke in a tongue and was using it, praying in another entirely different language, but I didn't know what it was, and I didn't know what mine was. Didn't matter, especially in that context as I later understood from studying the Bible in the months following. I did not firstly get (or need) a lesson on the doctrine of the Holy Spirit, unless to counter false or inadequate teaching I'd learned before. I was a blank slate, a white canvas. I needed the Saviour, and I needed power to witness. I got both within half an hour of each other. (I discovered later that this sort of shorter time frame was common in Acts).

For example, in Acts 8 the people had clearly heard the gospel and repented and got baptised. The evangelist Philip did not preach some half-baked gospel; as it makes clear, Philip 'proclaimed the good news', people 'were baptised' (8:12) they 'accepted the word of God' (8:14). Peter and John then later passed something else on to them: the filling (or 'receiving') of the Spirit. They needed power to witness, just as the first believers had at Pentecost, and following (Acts 2:1-4; 4:8 & 31). They needed to get, receive, take hold of the Spirit (8:15). The Spirit had not yet fallen on them, come on them, pressed upon them (8:16). Same Saviour; same Spirit. And like them, along with every new disciple we need the Saviour *and* ongoing power to witness. The record in Acts 8 is not simply some historically important event to show the gospel was for the Gentiles too. We all need the power of the Spirit. I was baptised with water as soon as possible. My testimony was like that of the group of people the Spirit suddenly fell on as Peter was speaking. They were baptised with water very soon after (Acts 10:44-48).

To finish, let me throw in another analogy. On one occasion I was about to lead a worship, teaching and prayer session on the Holy Spirit with a group of young people. One person in the group had arrived early to the church building where we were meeting. She wanted to cook something but did not know how to turn on the big oven in the kitchen. She called her father who knew how it worked (I did too, but she had already made the phone call, so I decided to say nothing and watch). Since I was about to teach on the Holy Spirit and pray for people my spiritual senses were on state of heightened alert; I sensed that God was going to give me a practical lesson I could also later share with the young people. I was all ears as the conversation and practical application followed.

'Dad, how do I turn on the oven?' she asked. He told her, and she followed his instructions. Inside there's what's called a pilot light, an initial, vital small flame in the oven. After that's been lit you have to hold down another knob for 30 seconds or so to enable the flame to expand across the bottom of the oven and so heat the whole thing up. Here's the analogy: Like the existence of the pilot light, every true believer *has* the Spirit of Christ, the Holy Spirit (Romans 8:9). But there's a subsequent filling, an empowering that is like heating up the entire oven stemming from that important initial flame. The inside gets engulfed. If the inside of that oven could have talked it would have certainly explained the difference. Same flame, just more of it. Same Spirit, just more of him, being filled and empowered in and by him, baptised, i.e. immersed in him.

That young woman's father was only too willing to tell her what to do. She couldn't see him, but she followed his instructions. How much more will our Father in heaven show us how to be filled, engulfed, having already had the flame of and presence of the Spirit put in our hearts after responding to the gospel.

It is not a matter of superiority or status; and it is something that happens to us, not merely an act of faith where nothing then happens. Or it can happen later on. I know people who have been filled with the Spirit by their bedside long after a meeting where people have prayed for them; while having a bath; while sitting on a bus; or at the back of a church meeting worshiping. Sometimes the Spirit suddenly comes upon them and no one else realises what is happening. Doesn't the story of Eldad and Medad teach us that God cannot be contained in a meeting or a meeting format? (Numbers 11). Check out verse 29. Are we not in that period now, the last days, the time from Jesus' ascension until his return?

It often involves the laying on of hands and is a very practical affair, like walking on water (put your foot out). Ask God to fill you. 'Open wide your mouth and he will fill it' (Psalm 81:10). Typically, it involves a release of the tongue as part of the empowerment, e.g. praise, prophecy, tongues. A study of the relevant passages in Acts (2, 8, 9, 10 & 19) where people were filled / baptised in the Spirit will yield fruit for any believer then willing to call on God to empower them, and others. Jesus Christ is the same yesterday, today and forever (Hebrews 13:8). Hallelujah!

ABOUT THE AUTHOR

FRASER (M.DIV., DENVER Seminary) has served on staff in churches in several countries. During that time he has recruited, encouraged and developed a number of young leaders. Some of his books reflect that continued interest in leadership development, while others are aimed at helping Christians more generally, or those curious about the Christian faith. Fraser currently lives in Scotland and has grown-up children, and several grandchildren.

Printed in Great Britain
by Amazon

74598698R00138